# CAULDRON

Jeff Dawson

# CAULDRON

# JEFF DAWSON

Jeff Dawson

Jeff Dawson

Mr. Dawson is the author of over eighteen works. His memoir, dedicated to his high school sweetheart, "Love's True Second Chance" was awarded the seal of approval from the IndiePendent Association for exemplary story writing. A full list can be found at the end of this work.

He currently lives in the Dallas/Fort Worth Area.

All the events describe did happen. In some cases, names of companies or individuals have been changed for personal privacy issues.

Jeff Dawson

Copyright © 2020 by: LDDJ Enterprises Publishing

ISBN: 978-1-7321547-5-9

All rights reserved, including the right to reproduce this book or portions thereof in any form or by any means, electronic or mechanical, including photocopying, recording, or by any information storage and retrieval system without permission in writing from the author. All inquiries should be addressed to LDDJ Enterprises Publishing, 1055 Regal Row #314, Dallas, TX. 75247.

## Table of Contents

1) SET-UP — 11
2) TRAINING — 13
3) KILYZAR — 20
4) KRAKOW — 25
5) SS COLONEL RUDOLPH GOUGH — 34
6) MEETING — 41
7) NICOLE AND DMITIRI — 45
8) MOSCOW — 49
9) UNIVERMAG — 52
10) OPERATION URANUS — 57
11) CAULDRON — 64
12) SNIPING — 78
13) ROSTOV-ON-DON — 83
14) THOUGHTS — 95
15) OTTO — 102
16) HUNTING GROUNDS — 106
17) CAPTURE — 116
18) THE BREWERY — 123
19) RETRUNING HOME — 140
20) DECISION — 149
21) PANZERS — 156
22) BEZPIECZENSTWO — 172
23) COLLAPSE — 175
24) ABANDONED — 187
25) NIKOLI — 191
26) FINAL ACT — 201
27) WESTWARD — 203
28) KHARKOV — 212
29) ACOUNTABILITY — 214

## THE CLANS

## BOIRARSKY

**Gregori-Ravina**

**Galina-Josif**

**Kirilli-Sasha**

**Dmitri-Roman-Sergei-Darya-Eva-Zoya**

## ROMANOV

**Marco**

**Ivan-Paulina**

**Nikoli-Svetlana**

**Konstantin-Irina**

**Stephan-Nicole-Yakov-Taras-Natashia-Dina-Elizabeth-Boris**

Jeff Dawson

# Chapter 1

# Set-Up

November 19th, 1942. General Georgy Zhukov was preparing to launch "Operation *Uranus*." He would unleash over a million men, fourteen thousand artillery pieces, and nine hundred tanks on the flanks of the 6th Army.

The German commander, General von Paulus, had no idea of the impending counterattack. He was focused on defeating the last pockets of Chuikov's army.

The 6th Army had been campaigning for over six months without a break. One more push and they could win this bitter battle. One more attack and they could raise the swastika over the ruins of this once majestic industrial town. One more battle and they would earn the right to rest, refit, and look back on a successful campaign. They never envisioned that it would not be they who would be victorious. The thought of their army being encircled and annihilated was an impossibility.

But of more consequence, they could not begin to imagine the horrors that would befall many of their brethren from an enemy they never saw.

\* \* \*

General Chuikov's men were fighting valiantly. They had held off attack after attack by the Germans who were getting closer each day to eradicating his dwindling forces. Several times Georgy asked him if von Paulus and his 6th Army were being drawn deeper and deeper into the depths of the bombed-out city. Chuikov assured him it was happening and that if he did not receive help soon, his forces would soon run out of room to fall back on and would themselves be stranded on the West bank of the Volga Until then, he and his men would continue the struggle and put up the staunchest resistance against the fascists to ensure the survival of the Motherland. He assured Chuikov he would continue to feed him enough reinforcements to achieve his stalling defensive action.

For months the Luftwaffe and artillery batteries rained bombs on the beleaguered defenders hoping they would succumb, die, or both. What they did not realize is that with each bomb dropped, they were creating hundreds of defensible hiding places that could not be destroyed from the air or continuous artillery bombardment. They would have to be taken, murderous meter by murderous meter.

This was not the type of warfare the Wehrmacht trained for—urban warfare. They were masters at Blitzkrieg tactics. Armored and motorized units would encircle the objectives ensuring all escape routes were closed and any counterattacks were repelled. The Luftwaffe would destroy concentrated troop build-ups, communication centers, major traffic crossings, and supply depots. The infantry would then catch up and eliminate any pockets of stubborn resistance.

Von Paulus knew the strategy of the past was worthless in this situation. The Russians were dug in, and the only way to appease Hitler and obtain the victory he so desperately wanted would require his men to weed out and kill every single one of the enemy.

He surveyed the smoldering city hoping this last rush would force Chuikov's rats to come to reason and surrender. If this final push succeeded, the Russian would be slaughtered and pushed into the Volga. If not…he couldn't think of that. Victory was at hand. It was time for him to rally the troops and convince them this would be the last battle.

# Chapter 2

# Training

## Romanovka

Svetlana and her girls had not eaten in over a week. She knew the trek would be difficult, but not this arduous. In order to keep her girls alive, she allowed them to feed on her. With her strength dissipating, she feared for their survival and hers.

It was four months since Nikoli banished them. Her anger and hatred for him fueled her for the first month. Any animal, soldier, or peasant she came across was disposed of. In some cases, she would take the time for her and Dina to feed on the prey. Most of the time, she would see Nikoli's face and kill the victim with an untold fury, spreading its remains over the ground. Dina and Elizabeth would try to feed off the scraps; Svetlana told them to keep moving.

The farther south they traveled the selection of game and wildlife diminished. She could hear the animals of the forest but none came close enough to be caught. She swore during some of the failed hunting attempts she heard faint laugher drifting in the treetops. Many times she found herself screaming into the forest for whatever was mocking her to show itself. The laughter only increased with each failed attempt. What she did not realize is each useless outburst was draining strength she could ill afford to lose. The strain and exhaustion finally caught up to her. She struggled to gain her breath, wishing her life would have been different. She cursed Nikoli for changing her even though she agreed to his demands. If she would have been stronger, she would not be trudging around in the forests with two children who were bleeding her dry. She raised herself from the ground, deciding that if she were going to die, she would do it on her feet, fighting.

"Let us go forward, girls. I am sure I will find some game before long."

\* \* \*

Another four agonizing hours passed with no luck. There was no game to be found. There were no more reserves to call upon. She was on the brink of giving up when she spotted a small shed a hundred meters ahead.

"Girls, we must rest for the night."

"Why?" asked Elizabeth in a hard tone.

"Because I said so."

They pushed open the door. The one-room hut was empty with the exception of one chair and a worn blanket. Svetlana collapsed to the floor. Dina fell on her knees next to her.

"Mother. Mother," Dina called out. "If you die, what will we do?"

"For once, my child, I do not know." Her eyes fluttered as she hovered between consciousness and the unknown.

"Of course, she does not know. She is only full of lies and hatred. I will provide for us."

Svetlana struggled to sit up. "You will do nothing of the sort! I am still in charge and will continue making the decisions for our group."

"And how will you accomplish that, Mother? Will you crawl on your knees to your prey? Perhaps you will convince the peasants you are a cripple and they will take pity on you. Is that your plan?" She let out a shrill laugh.

"NO!" cried Dina.

"Elizabeth." Svetlana struggled to her feet. "As long as I am alive, you will do as your—" Her body flew through the air crashing into the clay wall then slumped to the floor, unconscious.

Elizabeth walked over and stood above her mother. "Dina, from now on you will follow my desires and wishes. If not, you will share her fate."

"Elizabeth, you cannot kill Mother. Without her, we will have no guidance or path."

"We do not have one now. It is time we struck out on our own."

Dina moved to her mother's side. "I will not follow you. I would rather die beside Mother than take direction from you, you half-breed."

Dina didn't feel the right fist that knocked her out.

Elizabeth stood over the bodies contemplating how to end them.

"What a fitting end to two worthless individuals. I will suck them dry then remove their feeding tooth and leave. No one will know."

A blast of wind burst into the hut pinning her to the wall.

"You will not!" barked a voice. "I did not help your mother survive your birth so you could discard her as you wish. No, I have plans for all three of you."

'Who are you?" she spat out.

"The one who allows you to exist and the one who can and will kill you."

Rather than heed his words, she lunged at him. He caught her by the neck as she flew at him. "You have much to learn. Lesson number one—do not attack the one who took you in and kept you alive." He threw down two wolves from his left hand toward Dina.

"Little one, eat while I tend to your sister."

He directed his attention back to Elizabeth. "Lesson two—never give your opponent a second chance." He squeezed her neck harder until her face turned a dark blue.

"Three. Show your enemies no mercy." He struck her face hard, knocking her out then laid her beside Svetlana.

He turned to walk out the door then stopped. "Little one."

Dina did not look up as she was filling her starved veins. "Tell your mother nothing. I will return in a fortnight."

As he exited, the only sound was the sucking of blood and flesh from the dead animals.

**Two Days Later**

"Dina, I will only ask you one more time, who came to help us?"

"Mother, I have told you many times, he told me not to say."

"Why?"

"All I know is that if it were not for him, we would still be starving."

"That is not the point. I need to know if it is friend or foe."

A blast of cold wind blew open the door. In it stood a familiar figure holding two fresh corpses. He threw them to the floor then entered.

"I am neither. I am here to collect a debt."

"Who are you and what do you want?" quired Svetlana.

The man came closer. "Look into my eyes and tell me you do not remember."

She looked hard into his lifeless black eyes. "You!"

"Yes, my dear, it is I. I must say, I am having second thoughts about helping with the birth. Perhaps it would have been better if both of you had died and my clansmen raised the young one. It appears she is the only one who knows how to accept gratitude."

Svetlana looked about the room. "Where's Elizabeth?"

"What do you care?"

"She is my daughter and my thoughts about her are not of your concern."

"That is where you are wrong. Like your ancestors before you, when help is rendered, a debt is incurred that will be repaid. If not, those who are helped are given one option—death."

"I owe you—"

She found herself three feet off the floor looking into eyes filled with fire, death, and floating souls. "I tire of arguing with you and your kind. For whatever reason, you seem to think your species is indestructible. I assure you; it is not. I also assure you that dying from a broken feeding tooth or multiple untreatable wounds has many advantages over the death I will provide. If you still do not believe me, look closer then tell me how you wish to proceed."

What she saw scared the living hell out of her:

1) Bodies being drawn and quartered, sewn back together, and repeated.

2) Bodies burned beyond recognition, regenerated, and burned again

3) Souls ripped out of bodies and replaced, to be repeated

4) Beheadings by the hundreds. The heads sewn on other bodies, and the process repeated.

She could deal with the torture, but it was the screams from the victims that plagued her. The victims begged for mercy before the next horrible act was committed on them, only to be met with laughter from their tormentors. Their screams were earth-shattering and long. The pain on their faces was indescribable. She was convinced to listen.

"The payment is simple. Our country has been infested with a pestilence that must be eradicated. I could call on my people to end the invasion, but we agreed, hundreds of years ago, humans must deal with the inherent problems the constantly place themselves in."

She heard a shot ring out from the woods.

"I am going to teach you and your daughters the art of sniper warfare."

"Why do we need to learn such an art?"

"Because I am telling you, you will learn. Or do you prefer the alternative?"

She pondered the proposal for a few seconds.

"When do we start?"

"Immediately."

\* \* \*

The next three weeks was a time for learning and bonding. He took the girls out every day instructing them how to be proficient with the Mosin-Nagant rifle. Each night they were forced to break the weapon down, clean it, then rebuild it. If any of them complained, he would have them look into his eyes for clarification on why they were doing this.

Elizabeth excelled at concealment when in the open. Dina became the most proficient in hitting targets. Svetlana was the master at range determination and locations for firing positions.

When they failed an assignment, the penalty was no feeding on fresh kills. If they were hungry, they could look to each other.

The tactic forced them to work together and overlook any deficiencies each one exhibited. For the first time in her life, Svetlana was starting to understand the term, *Comrade*. She had heard the term but never put much stock in it. The comradery that interested her was getting what she wanted no matter who was destroyed or left out of her plans. She found herself revisiting the passing of Stephan more than she let on. Her rage at his death was no longer out of control. She was learning how to harness it and turn it to her advantage. She also found herself becoming emotionally attached to her girls. They were no longer mouths to feed or tolerate—they were becoming her comrades in arms.

"You three have done well. I am pleased. It is now time for you to leave and head to your destination and help those who fight for the Motherland to ensure our victory. However, if you fail, we will meet again."

A rush of cold air ripped into the single room and he was gone.

The girls turned to their mother. "Shall we?"

"Yes. It is time to prove our worth."

# Chapter 3

# Kilyzar

Konstantin was pleased with the damage they inflicted at Kharkov. It would be months before the station would operate efficiently. It was time to turn his attention to other matters. He watched the German drive to the Caucasus Mountains with great interest. If they were successful, they could effectively seal off the main oil supply to the rest of the country. What interested him most was the drive to Stalingrad. He understood the tactical importance of the move, but also saw a significant weakness in the overall plan. If Zhukov could muster the forces, he could launch a counterattack toward Rostov-on-Don and seal off the German units in the south. That would be a major victory for any general.

Another idea he was pondering was the fast-moving machines referred to as tanks. The Germans proved their excellent mobility with the launch of the Russian invasion. It was perfected around Kiev when over 600,000 men were encircled by the armored units. He knew that to survive, one must learn to adapt. It was time to learn how to fight with new weapons and tactics.

\* \* \*

Konstantin called all the members for a planning session. They were gathered around the table waiting for him. When he entered the room he could not help but notice the members were still clinging to old principles: jealousy, mistrust and suspicion. They were still operating as individuals and not a collective. *Perhaps time will change this. If not, it will make our task that much more difficult.* He took his place at the head of the table.

"I want to congratulate everyone on a job well done. I believe it is safe to say, despite a few injuries and the loss of one of our own, our mission was a complete success. It will be months before adequate supplies can be funneled through the railyard at Kharkov, thus making resupply to the advancing units difficult. Do not think though that the battle has been won. The Germans are still advancing and killing our fellow countrymen by the thousands. While our methods are sound, it is time for us to branch out and embrace the new technology both armies are using—tanks. I propose we borrow a few of these weapons, with their crews, and learn how they work."

Boris and Kirilli stared in shocked silence. They looked at each other with blank stares then back at Konstantin.

"What? No one has a word to say? Irina? Sasha? Boris? Kirilli? Anything?"

The members glanced back and forth at each other.

"Surely someone has something to say about my brilliant plan."

"Is that what you call it? Brilliant? I call it suicidal," said Boris. "In all the centuries we have served together I have never heard of a more preposterous idea. You cannot be serious? We have proven our worth with time-honored practices. I see no reason to lower our standards and fight on the human level."

Konstantin let out a laugh. "My old friend. Have you not forgotten why we became pirates? We thought we were living a full life, feeding and taking what we wanted when we deserved it. But it left us hamstrung and confined. It was not until we learned to sail ships that we increased our wealth. If not for our pirate days, I would not have met my lovely wife, Irina."

"Back then we had a purpose. I will agree your idea to learn seamanship added to our wealth and standing, but I see no benefit with your current idea."

"I agree with Boris," Kirilli chimed in. "To what gain will be accomplished? As a financier and businessman, I see no advantage."

"Anyone else have a comment? Irina? Sasha? Have the ladies nothing to add before I explain my reasons?"

"Husband, I have always followed your lead, but I agree with Boris and Kirilli. What can possibly be gained?"

"Interesting point. Sasha? Anything to add?"

She was still bristling with being used at Kharkov. "You used me once. I do not intend to let it happen again. Your idea is foolish. We are vampires. We hunt and stalk and take what we want. You will not have my support!"

He walked over to Sasha. "Let me remind you, my dear, I used you so we would not fail. If you find that distasteful, so be it. It served our purpose and eliminated a foe I had been hunting for several decades. Plus, I would never think of putting your pretty, soft ass in such a vehicle. It would demean the weapon of its fierce fighting capabilities."

She attempted to rise from her chair; he thrust her back down.

"Take your hands off my wife, Konstantin!"

"Or what? What will you do?"

"I will make you regret the day you laid hands on her!"

Konstantin roared with laughter. "The great Kirilli speaks. Good. This is good." He backed away.

"Roman, do you have any insight to my current idea?"

"I think it is an excellent idea. Our tactics have been successful, but we must look to the future. The use of these weapons could help us cause more damage and confusion to our enemies."

"Excellent. Excellent! The boy can be taught. This is exactly why I am proposing this idea. We can maximize our destruction of the enemy forces with their own weapons. Does anyone disagree with this?"

It was a few moments before Boris spoke. "How do you propose we do this?"

"We will capture and convert two to four crews. They will teach us everything we need to know on how to operate and maintain the machines. We must be careful when we take them. Damaging their uniforms must be avoided at all costs. They will have IDs and possibly orders that will benefit us in the future such as allowing them into refitting and refueling stations."

"And just how do you propose to capture them?" asked Sasha sarcastically. "Let me guess. You are going to walk up to the unit's commander and demand he do as he is told."

"Not exactly, but you are close. Once we have located our targets, we will use the tactics that served you all so well in the beginning. You, Irina, Natashia, Kladviya, Darya, and Zoya will use your womanly charms to distract the men. Once they are occupied the rest of us will make our entrance."

"I am not going anywhere with that bitch, Kladviya," shouted Natashia. "I would rather die than serve with her."

He flashed to her side, picked her up, and slammed her on the table. "Let me know when you want your wish granted."

Sasha, Irina, Kirilli, and Boris came to her rescue. The women grabbed his arms and twisted them behind his back. Boris restrained his legs. Kirilli used his hands as a vise on his head.

"Enough!" yelled Kladviya. "Father, this is getting us nowhere. Attacking her will only force her to fight harder to win the affections of Roman. In time, she and I will have our own battle. Until then, we need to concentrate on your proposal."

He shrugged himself from his prisoners. "My daughter is wiser than I thought. She speaks the truth." He went back to his chair and sat down.

"When do we go?" inquired Boris.

"As soon as possible."

"Where do you think we will find enough tanks to implement the plan?"

"Rostov-on-Don," answered Roman. "Many of the guards in Kharkov talked about the 4th Panzer Army being stationed there. That is my suggestion."

Konstantin scanned the room. "Anyone else?" No one answered. "Good. We leave for the city tomorrow."

## Chapter 4

## Krakow

Nikoli spent his entire life trying to be a man of great renown and courage. Yet when faced with adversity, he crumbled. It was time for him to do something he always avoided—lead. Unlike his past battles, there would be no one to blame if the plan he was developing failed; there would be no Kirilli, Roman, Svetlana, or Konstantin to blame. He would shoulder the entire burden.

\* \* \*

"How do you propose getting into the camp?" asked Schmidt.

"Based on the security and detail I encountered at Wewelsburg, it will be necessary to obtain transportation. Even though I still have papers from Himmler, I doubt they will get us into the camp." He shocked himself with the revelation. "Papers. We are going to need authentic orders to gain entrance. Any ideas?"

Schmidt paced back and forth for a moment. "What about Jacub? I'm sure if he cannot do it, he would know who to contact."

Nikoli leaned back in his chair. "True, but there is one problem. He is currently stationed in the camp."

"He is, but that does not mean he is living on-site. Employees are either housed off-site in barracks, or they are occupying a dwelling close to the compound."

"Interesting. We could get to him if he is off-site. If they have him living inside the wire, we will have to think of something else. Let me ponder that. Back to transportation. Are you a qualified staff car driver?"

"I am. My main assignment when not pulling guard duty at the rail station was transporting the vermin in lorries from their homes to the station."

"You understand a car is different than a lorry?"

"Nikoli, you test my patience. Even though I am a vampire, not by choice, I am also a well-trained German soldier capable of many duties. Mastering the gears of a staff car will take no more than five minutes."

"Excellent. Excellent."

"I do see one problem?"

"And that would be?"

"The staff car. Unless I am mistaken, we do not have one on hand."

"True. True. When we go scout Jacub's quarters we will also take note of the local traffic."

"And do what?"

"Establish how we will obtain one."

"This will be interesting."

"Are you mocking me?"

"Not at all. Only pointing out that I doubt they will let us walk up and take one."

"Of course not, you fool. It will take planning. If you are finished let me get back to the plan. A uniform. Yours is much too worn and weathered to be accompanying an SS Colonel."

He looked at his worn, bloodstained tunic. "It could use an upgrade."

"Indeed. I do not think it will be a problem to find a replacement. The trick will be for us to show restraint when obtaining it."

"Agreed."

Nikoli stood up, stretched, then walked toward the door. "Tomorrow we begin to scout."

**Two Days Later**

Nikoli and Schmidt sat under a tree a few thousand meters from the camp.

"We are fortunate; Jacub is living outside the wire. The only problem is the guard assigned to him. Why do you think he needs one?"

"Nikoli, it is standard procedure to guard an administrator in the camp. If you notice, anyone who leaves does not go alone."

"What is the reason for this?"

"Security."

"Security?"

"Yes. Did you never notice all the guards at the railway station? Did you really think they were all there for the prisoners?"

"I never put much thought to it." He paused for a minute, laughing. "As I was getting what I wanted, what did I care?"

"You should have been more attentive. Half of the guards were there to guard the guards."

"Why?"

"For the last time—security. Did you ever see anyone try to escape at the station?"

"Yes."

"And what happened to them?"

"They were shot."

"Correct. And then the body was disposed of in a way no one would ever find them."

"Burned?"

"Or buried in lime off the beaten path. They cannot take the chance that Jacub might have a change of mind and decide not to return to work. If his knowledge of what is going on behind the wire became known to our enemies, it could weaken the war effort."

"I see. Regardless, he is still a problem."

They both mulled the issue over for a moment.

"We have no choice," said Nikoli. "We must convert the guard. He would still perform his daily duties, but we would have to make sure he obeyed Jacub."

"Will he not prove to be a problem?" asked Schmidt.

"Not necessarily. Is he the only guard that watches over Jacub?"

"Yes."

"Where does he stay when off duty?"

"In the same building as Jacub."

"Excellent. How often does he check in?'

"Once a week a sergeant comes to check on him."

"Perfect. When I convert him, I will instruct him to follow Jacub's orders while still obeying his superior. The last item is hiding the bite marks." Schmidt pulled down his collar, exposing his marks.

"We will treat them like any wound with mud and water., To help conceal the holes, we will cut jagged lines hole-to-hole. That should help."

"Excellent idea. Have you figured out the transportation issue?"

"Yes. While you observed Jacub's movements, I revisited Krakow taking notes of the military traffic. There is an inordinate amount of staff cars parked by the Gestapo headquarters. Many of them are not being used and are only lightly guarded. We will get a car and your new uniform without a problem."

"You have thought this out well."

"Perhaps. The only thing I cannot predict is how Jacub will respond. Threatening him with death would be pointless as we saw at our last encounter. This would be an excellent job for Kirilli."

"Kirilli? Surely you jest."

He turned on Schmidt emitting sparks of fire from his eyes. "Despite my past behavior toward him, that does not mean I did not learn from him. He is an excellent orator and knows exactly what words to use. I hope I can do the same."

"When shall we go?"

"Tonight."

\* \* \*

The lone guard never heard the men approaching him. The first hint he was not alone was the sensation of razors slashing into his neck.

"What shall we do with him now?"

Nikoli surveyed the grounds. "Put him on the back side of the house. He will be out for at least an hour; plenty of time to take care of our business."

Jacub was sitting at his table, pouring himself another stiff drink. His months of working for Major Klaus Richter were taking a terrible toll. He almost missed the days when Nikoli would storm into his office threatening him with his very life. Death would have been a welcomed visitor. It took a few weeks to realize what his new job entailed. He was told it was a selection position. Those who could perform manual, rigorous labor would be assigned to one part of the camp while those better suited for domestic duties would go to another sector. It seemed harmless at first. Within a few weeks, he discovered the true nature of his position. Those chosen for hard labor did exactly that; they worked until their skin wrapped around their bones, and their eyes bulged from their sockets. Those sent for domestic duties were stuffed into overcrowded barracks infested with lice and typhus. Those who didn't succumb to disease or starvation were sent to the block houses where the ovens were in operation. The thought of sending his fellow man, woman or child to death was unconscionable.

He thought many times of trying to kill himself, but his jailers made sure there were no implements available for him to perform the rash action. The one thing they did supply was an ample cache of liquor.

A loud knock at the door brought him to his senses.

"What do you want?" he yelled out.

"Entrance, old friend."

The voice was familiar, yet he couldn't place it.

"I ask again, what do you want and why are you not talking to the guard? I am a busy man."

"I fear your companion is not able to comply."

The fog began clearing from his mind. *Nikoli? What the hell would he be doing here?*

"Old friend," came the voice. "Are you going to leave us out in the cold or allow us to enter?"

He rose from the chair, regrouped his composure then walked to the door

"Nikoli?"

"It is I, old friend."

*Nikoli never addressed me in such a tone or words. It must be a trick.*

"How do I know it is actually you? The Nikoli I know has never used a kind word in his life."

Nikoli's patience was getting thin. "Because, you fat, useless sack of meat, if you do not open the door, I will break it down and suck every last drop of blood from your body."

*It is Nikoli.*

He opened the door and retreated to the table.

Nikoli and Schmidt entered, closing the door behind them.

"Is that any way to greet an old friend?"

"I have no friends. I have no soul. I only wish to drink till I die."

Nikoli took a good look at Jacub. This was not the man he knew. His weight must have been down to forty-seven kilos. He no longer had any strands of hair on his head, and his skin was much paler than normal.

"I would ask how you are doing, but I can see the answer."

"Thank you for noticing." He took another drink. "Why are you here and what do you want?"

"I need your help."

"What did you say? The great Nikoli needs my help! That is laughable. I guess the next words I hear will be, 'I have always liked you, Jacub.' Please, leave me to my misery and shame."

Nikoli was running out of soothing words. The Jacub he knew was hardly a man to be dealt with. He was a sniveling, weak bureaucrat, but when pushed would attempt to push back. What sat before him was a shell of the previous man he knew, physically. Mentally, Jacub was displaying a nasty, sarcastic spirit he was unaccustomed to.

"Jacub, I need you to listen to me."

"Why?"

Schmidt walked up to him and slapped his face.

"Because, you sniveling fool, he told you to!" He raised his right hand to strike him again.

"NO!" bellowed Nikoli. "Touch him again and you will feel my wrath!"

Schmidt backed up a few steps.

Nikoli reached out and placed his hands on Jacub. "I need your help."

"Schmidt and I need to gain entrance to the camp." He pulled his hands back.

"Why?"

"We need to reconnoiter the camp."

He was becoming intrigued. "Why?"

"We are going to break in and attempt to liberate as many of the prisoners as possible."

He shook his head. "You are going to do what?"

"We are going to break in and liberate prisoners."

He reached to take another drink. Nikoli stopped him. "I need your help, Jacub."

"I do not understand why. You could easily break in with your clan and kill everyone you want."

"That might have been true in the past, but what you see in front of you is all that is left."

"Are you telling me Svetlana, Dina, Roman, Kirilli, Sasha, and the others have disowned you?"

"Something like that, yes."

Jacub broke out in hysterical laughter. "I cannot believe my ears. The great Nikoli has been banished. Oh, please. Tell me more."

He could take the insults and pressure no more. Blood began seeping from his fingernails, ears, and eye sockets. His jawline began contorting making room for the feeding incisors. His voice became harsh and hoarse.

"I came here as a friend. I should have known better." His voice became louder. "I should have killed you years ago just to satisfy my own thirst and disgust of a useless man such as yourself. Since you are not willing to help me, then you are of no use to me!" Green fire began sparking in his eyes. The room began filling with the roaring sound of bones and muscles stretching and twisting as he and Schmidt transformed.

Jacub knew he only had seconds to make a wise decision. As much as he wished for death, he did not want it to be at the hand of two vampires.

"I will help, Nikoli," he yelled. "I will help!"

"A wise choice my old friend," growled the voice. "A wise choice."

Schmidt went out to check on the guard while Nikoli told Jacub his plan. It would take at least a week to secure the required papers. To signal Nikoli that everything was ready, he would set one a potted plant in the windowsill.

The last detail was the guard. Nikoli treated the wounds with mud and water. They began healing immediately. The only problem would be feeding him since normal food would not satisfy his hunger.

"Jacub, he must feed at least once every two days. Three if possible but not desired."

"What will he feed on? I have no food here. All the meals are taken at the canteen."

Nikoli looked at him.

"That is impossible. He cannot feed on me. I will become….one of…you."

"Would that be such a bad thing?"

"Right now, yes."

"My friend, as long you do not struggle it will be painless, and you will not be turned unless you request it, I promise."

He thought about the proposition. "Promise?"

"Promise."

"Very well. I will cooperate."

"Excellent. Then it is time for us to leave. We will keep a watchful eye for the sign." He glanced outside making sure the area was still secure. "Schmidt, it is time."

Both men headed for the door.

"Nikoli. One last item."

He turned to look at Jacub.

"Kirilli would be proud."

He smiled. "Thank you." Then slammed the door shut.

# Chapter 5

# SS Colonel Rudolph Gough

## Carinhall

He watched with great interest as Adolf Hitler rose through the ranks of the Nazi party and began uniting a fractured country. The man promised great things for all the German people: stature, jobs, prosperity, idealism, a new national pride, and most important, the rebuilding of the military. They would ignore the Versailles Treaty and rearm their great nation. They would become a world power once again. That is what intrigued him the most.

He cared not for the common people. Every country had them and needed them, but why so many? Why did governments not fine those who continued to produce offspring who never contributed to society but insisted society should take care of them? They were all leeches, and he despised them with a passion. The world needed more people like he and his family.

The patriarchs of the family had toiled for decades building up their wealth and holdings in commodities and real estate. It didn't matter that many of the properties they took over were by nefarious means. If the original owners would have been wiser in their investments and property management, they would still be in possession of the lands. But there was a price to pay for their wealth that they embraced and the state sponsored—military service.

His grandfather Heinz, and father Walter, had proudly donned the uniform of the day and served the men in charge.

Heinz was on the General Staff with Otto von Bismarck and helped in the uniting of what would become modern Germany. His father served under Wilhelm Kaiser in the Great War that had brought about the current dilemma for his country. It swayed him none. When his father returned home after the armistice was signed, he informed young Rudolph that many countries experienced setbacks. This was one of those times. But it too would pass. Before he left Berlin, he met with a few old friends, who assured him the family holdings were not in jeopardy, and that his son would still receive the proper training at the prestigious Prussian Military Academy.

He graduated top of his class in 1924 excelling on the rifle range. Even though it was difficult to purchase arms and ammunition after the war, his father always managed to show up with an ample supply. He convinced the shopkeepers the bullets were for hunting and sport, nothing else. Sport was a loose term. No one knew of the numerous human targets scattered across the estate. Walter told him such a gift must not be wasted. It should be honed on every occasion. At first Rudolph questioned the wisdom of shooting his fellow countrymen until his father convinced him they were a drag on the economy. They had no hope, no life, no job. Thus, they were doing them a favor by ending their miserable useless lives. Rudolph never gave it another thought when he pulled the trigger.

Many times, his father would walk into his room with the words, "It is time to hunt." He would grab his rifle, knapsack, bedroll, canteen, and one change of clothing. Many of the excursions lasted weeks: winter, spring, summer, fall. It did not matter. "Son, you will not be able to choose the time or place when your time comes to serve. Therefore, you must be ready for all possible eventualities."

The most painful trip was in February of '32. He'd been stalking a deer for four days. It was a majestic beast—a sixteen-point buck. He visualized replacing the fourteen-point his father had hanging over the fireplace filled him with pride.

He knew the buck would be entering the clearing two hundred meters away. The blind he built kept him well out of sight. As the sun cleared the trees, the buck came into his sight. He could see steam pouring out of its nostrils as it scratched for food. He took a deep breath, slid his finger around the trigger, slowly exhaled, and pulled the trigger. The bullet impacted in one second, bursting its heart. He cleaned the animal as his father taught him, built a small sled, and headed home. That is when the hunt took a turn for the worse.

When he came to the stream, he had crossed hundreds of times, he miscalculated how thick the ice was. Halfway across, it broke. His right ankle snapped when it struck a rock. His father always told him "adversity is when you learn." With no one to call out to for help, he pulled himself out of the icy water, put together a makeshift splint, and continued home with his prize.

By the second day, the pain was becoming intense. He tried numbing the pain by packing snow around his ankle. He also knew he could lose his foot if he did not get proper medical attention soon. The worst part was the howls he heard each night. They were getting closer and closer to him. The wolves were searching for him and his prize. He vowed not to give in; he would rather die than succumb.

On the third day, it appeared his wish was going to happen. He awoke in a daze from the pain and the cold. He could make out at least six wolves thirty meters out and closing. He tried to raise his rifle but had not the strength. The solace he could console himself with was how proud his father would have been.

The wolves were now no more than fifteen meters away when several shots rang out. He thought he was dreaming until a voice brought him out of his stupor, "Rudolph, it is time to go home."

Rather than ask how his father knew how to find him, he asked, "Father, what of the deer?"

"Son, it is a majestic animal, one you can be proud of bringing down, but in warfare, we do not always get to take home our rightful gains. Remember this. You will always know you bagged one larger than your father."

It took two months for him to recover from the broken ankle and frostbite damage. The doctor was able to save everything but his left index finger. It would be a reminder that even the best plans can go awry.

When Hitler took power, with help from his father, he resigned from the Wehrmacht and joined the Liebstandarte SS Adolf Hitler. He was accepted into the elite division in 1936.

At first, he was enamored with the rallies the party held. Never had he seen such pride and nationalism from the masses. When he spoke to his father of the Führer's magnetic personality and the hope he was giving the people, he only replied, "Son, leaders come and go. Governments rise and fall. The only constant a man can rely on are duty, honor, integrity, and courage."

When he saw what was coming, he knew that being on the outside was not for him. He would need to prove his worth to his country and himself.

He was assigned to a scouting party. Their mission was to find the enemy, report back to headquarters, then return to the front where they would practice their craft.

He did more than practice—he perfected his skill. Each and every kill was logged in a special notebook for snipers. It was an impressive accounting of his activities: Poland 10 kills, Holland 15, France 40, Greece 20. These were the ones he logged as they represented targets of opportunity that could alter a battle: officers, machine-gunners, sentries, etc. He chose not to log in the occasional peasant he shot.

Unlike animals, humans were not predictable. He would loose off a round to warn them they were being hunted. Then the fun would begin. He would toy with them by deliberately revealing his position and breaking a large branch or imitating a bird call. It was the panic in their eyes he could see through the scope that triggered the adrenaline rush. Like all hunts they must come to an end, and even though he regretted ending the fun, there was other prey awaiting his eyes. He lined up the victim, zeroed in, then pulled the trigger. With the rush over, he packed his rifle and returned to his quarters.

When he approached the gate, the sergeant on duty halted him.

"Sergeant, what is the meaning of this inconvenience? You know who I am. I am tired and ready to retire to the barracks."

"Colonel, you have a communique from Berlin. It is marked urgent."

"When did it arrive?"

"Two hours ago, Colonel."

"I see. Very well. Are you going to hand it over or do I have to hunt for it?"

He reached into the guard shack and produced the document.

"Thank you, sergeant. I will try and remember you in my report."

"Jawohl, Herr Colonel. Heil Hitler!"

"Heil, Hitler." he nonchalantly replied.

"Bastard."

He took off his overcoat, boots and unbuttoned his tunic. Poured a glass of brandy then opened the letter.

The order read –

*Colonel Rudolph Gough is on leave for six months or until his current commanding officer deems it necessary for him to return to the unit for active duty.*

He was reading the local paper, while enjoying a glass of Napoleon brandy when the phone rang.

* * *

"Pull," called Rudolph calmly.

The clay pigeons spread across the sky. He dropped every one without flinching.

Himmler and Goering watched in awe as their top sniper shot one hundred out of one hundred.

"Excellent, Herr Gough," remarked Himmler. "Someday you must teach us your technique."

He removed the spent shells and rested the gun on his left arm.

"Herr Himmler. It would be an honor, but I believe you have more important duties at this time."

"Indeed. In fact, that is why we called you here today."

"What may I do to serve my Fatherland?"

"We have a situation in Stalingrad that we believe requires your special skills."

"What would that be, if I may be so bold as to ask?"

"You may. I am sure you are aware of our current struggle in Stalingrad."

"I am. According to the papers, we will achieve final victory in a matter of weeks."

"Yes, that is true, but it appears the Russians have sent one of your counterparts to the city. We considered him a nuisance at first. That has changed."

"How?"

"He is targeting our officers and machine-gunners. Although these men are easily replaced, it is having an effect on morale."

"May I ask how bad?"

"Of course. Our men are making the best of it, but I, the Führer, and the Reichsführer agree that if we send you in, the problem will go away, and we will achieve our glorious victory."

"I see. When do I leave?"

"In a week if not sooner."

He walked over to his gun case and carefully wiped down his weapon before putting it in.

"Herr Himmler, I will be ready to leave in two days."

"Excellent." He took a pause. "One other thing."

"Yes."

"We are sending you an escort."

"Herr Himmler, with all due respect, I work alone. He will only slow me down."

"The request comes from the Führer himself. He is confident you can teach him your art which will only hasten our victory."

He snapped the case shut. "Very well. What is his name?"

"Codename, Otto."

# Chapter 6

# Meeting

**Stalingrad**
**West Bank of the Volga**

Chuikov studied the map detailing his forces and the Germans. The Tractor Works had fallen. The chemical plant was under siege. The Germans had reached the Volga to the north and south. His pocket of resistance was shrinking.

Most commanders would surmise resistance was futile, but for each meter of land he surrendered, he was able to consolidate his forces and rapidly move them to another area of concern. He was no longer faced with long lines of logistics and communication, unlike his foe.

The sound of exploding artillery shells could be heard in the distance as his enemy attempted another breakthrough. Piles of dust fell from the rafters, sprinkling his map. He smiled knowing that in the coming weeks his persistence and stubbornness would pay off.

"Comrade General, you have some visitors."

"Not now, Yuri."

"Comrade General, they insist."

"Yuri, I have no time for visitors. We are not running a hospitality center. Send them to a collection point, or even better, enlist them in one of the penal battalions."

Yuri's body flew past him, crashing into the earthen wall.

"Comrade General, they insist," he muttered.

Chuikov drew his pistol then turned to shoot the intruders. An iron hand clamped down on his right hand wrenching the pistol away.

It took a moment for his eyes to adjust to the figures standing before him. They were women, but not ordinary peasant girls. They carried an aura of authority and invincibility about them.

"Comrade General, my name is Svetlana Romanov and these are my girls, Dina and Elizabeth. We have been sent here to assist in defeating the Germans."

Chuikov regained his composure. "On whose orders?"

"A mutual friend, General Zhukov."

"I am aware of no such orders. I will have to verify what you say." He looked to Yuri as he was attempting to stand up. "Call headquarters and verify why these three wenches are here."

Yuri moved towards his wireless set. He found himself being knocked down again.

Svetlana moved to within a meter of Chuikov. "That will not be necessary. The only important information you need to verify is if we are friend or foe."

He sat down, keeping his stoic face intact. "I am listening."

"My daughters and I have been training for the last three months as snipers. We are ready to put our craft to the test."

"And how do you plan on doing that?"

"Any way we decide." Green fire flickered in her eyes. "The only request we have is for you and your troops to stay out of our way. We are here to help or impede. Any interference from you or your men will result in grave consequences." She looked over to Yuri as he again struggled to stand.

"Any questions?"

Chuikov's facial expression never changed. "I have no questions at this time. I only warn you that if you interfere with my plans, I will not be responsible for your safety."

"I did not ask you to concern yourself with our safety, did I? No. I told you to stay away."

"I do not know who you are nor do I care. I will tell you this though; I fear no man or beas—.

In the blink of an eye, Elizabeth and Dina surrounded him and raised him off his seat. Each one placed a hand around his throat.

Svetlana moved her face to within two centimeters from his. "Any other ill-timed comments? Or my daughters will rip you to shreds."

He forced out a, "No."

"Good. Girls, release him. We have work to do." They exited the headquarters.

"Comrade General, shall I notify Zhukov of this meeting?"

"No. Let them go. If the Germans do not kill them, the city will. Now, let us return to our daily assignments."

### Potsdam Railroad Station

Rudolph paced up and down the platform impatient to leave. The train was running fifteen minutes behind schedule. If there was one thing he abhorred it was tardiness. And this was no exception. He was irritated that Otto had not arrived yet. This was not the way to impress a man of his reputation and standing.

"Herr Gough," came a voice. "It is good to see you are prepared for the journey." He turned around to see Himmler, his bodyguard detail, and another man wearing the rank of major.

Let me introduce Major Otto Blümberg. He will be accompanying you to Stalingrad." Otto snapped his heels and gave the mandatory Nazi salute. Gough wasn't impressed yet he returned the salute. He then looked down at his watch.

"My apologies, Herr Gough. The train was delayed by my orders. It should be arriving any moment now." A whistle blew from the west.

"Herr Reichsführer. What are my orders concerning Otto?"

"In what matter, Herr Gough?"

"In regard to his duties once we arrive at our destination?"

"Do not trouble yourself with that. He knows what to do when you arrive."

"With all due respect, Herr Reichsführer, since he will be in my charge, I believe I have the right to know what his assignment is."

"Not true. Your orders are to get him to Stalingrad. Once you have arrived, he will no longer be your responsibility. He will report to General von Paulus."

The train pulled into the station puffing out great clouds of steam as the brakes were applied.

"Herr Colonel, your train is waiting."

Gough snapped to attention and clicked his heels. "Heil Hitler."

"Heil Hitler."

The two men boarded the train.

# Chapter 7

# Nicole and Dmitri

Dmitri was the perfect father for the first few months. He tended and cared for Nicole and the twins as a good father would. That was changing. Nicole became more demanding every day. It mattered not what he did; it was wrong in her eyes. Why had not Kirilli shared all of his knowledge in the care of a belligerent bride and demanding children? The few times they discussed the path Dmitri was taking, he would only shake his head and wish him well. Dmitri knew he heard him quietly laughing as he walked away. Perhaps this is what becoming a father and a vampiric man was all about? In time, he would sort this out.

Another issue weighing on his mind was feeding his clan. At first, it was not a problem. There was plenty of game and the occasional transient he would bring home. As time progressed, he was forced to go farther and farther out in search of food. Many times he came back empty-handed, forcing the twins to feed on him and Nicole. It was becoming unbearable. He must find a new food supply and fast.

To compound the problems, there was also another force nagging at him—conflict. He missed the missions. He missed going out on raids and killing Germans. At first, he was aghast at the revelation but became more comfortable with the thought each passing day. He needed to get back to where the action was.

"Dmitri! When are you going hunting again? The children and I are hungry. Do you hear me?"

He sat at the table cringing.

"Dmitri. Are you listening to me?"

He rose from the chair.

"I will not ask again! Answer me!"

He walked into the bedroom. His eyes bore into hers. "Woman, you will address me as husband from this day forward and you will address me in a civil tone."

"Or what?" she snapped back.

"Or I will do what Nikoli did to Svetlana."

A long pause filled the room. She placed the twins on the bed then approached him. "Or what? You have neither the demeanor or backbon—"

He grabbed both of her arms and threw her onto the bed. "I have more backbone than you can imagine. Testing my patience right now would not prove healthy for you. I have suppressed my feelings for you much too long. It is time I became a real man like my father and yours and build my own clan. In order for that to happen, we are going to leave this place and return to Bezpieczeństwo."

She sat up, regrouping herself. "I have no desire to ever return to that place. We are fine where we are at."

He turned his back on her. "Woman, you will do as I say. I am your husband, and what I say is what you will do."

He could feel the air becoming heavy. He knew what was coming and started changing in kind.

"My mother was right," came a hoarse response. "You are nothing but a sniveling, incompetent vampire imitating a man."

Blood poured from his nails and ears when he spun around. His bones and muscles crackled with the transformation. The twins began baying and screeching as their parents began turning.

"Your mother is and always will be a whore! Your father is not a leader. He is a spineless, cowardly individual who brings disgrace to the Romanov name!"

She was halfway changed and filling with rage at the insults. Reddish-green fire flashed through her eyes. "My father is a great leader. Yours is the one who is the mistake. Nikoli should have killed him when he had the chance instead of trying to teach him anything of importance. And you can leave my mother out of it. She is more of a man than you will ever be. If it were not for her, me and my children would have starved!"

His change was almost complete. Even though his vocal cords were becoming constricted, she could make out his words. "Your mother is a whore. Your father is a coward, and you are nothing more than a spoiled whore-to-be!"

The children were now howling uncontrollably as their parents flew at each other.

Fur and blood erupted into the air as they clawed and tore at each other. He bit hard into her left shoulder and she sunk her teeth deep in his neck. They both screamed with the wounds, but neither would yield.

They continued their onslaught. Clumps of fur, hair, and blood erupted in the air as they continued striking each other. Their howls shook the timbers of the hut.

Dmitri wrapped his massive arms around Nicole in a death grip. She performed the same move. Each struggled for breath as they attempted to squeeze each other to death. For a split second, they looked into each other's eyes. They were abysses of black hatred. Dmitri could feel her ribs cracking. He squeezed harder; another crack. Nicole flung her head backward, letting out a terrifying cry as she tried to crack his.

Her exposed neckline was what he had been waiting for. He could end her life now and be done with her. Instead of going for the veins, he sank his incisors just below them then penetrated her with his hard member.

She screamed with pleasure as he entered her. He thrust her up and pinned her against the wall as they mated.

**Six hours later.**

Nicole woke up first. She went outside, grabbed a bucket of water and mixed dirt in it. She returned and started dressing his wounds. He stirred with her movements, grabbing her arm.

"Woman, what are you doing?"

"Dressing your wounds, husband."

He carefully watched her spread the mixture on his chest.

"And the children?"

"Resting. I was able to find a few foxes this morning."

He grunted as she applied the salve.

"About yesterday, my wife."

"Think nothing of it. I was just as guilty." She winked. "Husband, when do we leave?"

He leaned up and kissed her. "When our wounds heal."

# Chapter 8

# Moscow

### November 3rd

Zhukov walked over to the window, glancing at the weather reports he received that morning. They were promising but not what he had hoped for. He gazed out, examining the partly cloudy sky. *General Winter* was making him sweat.

He was building up a massive force east of the Volga out of the range of the Luftwaffe's prying eyes. His *Night Witches* were proving their worth harassing German forward positions and keeping the anti-aircraft crews on high alert, leaving them little time for sleep. They were also frustrating the meager fighter force Goering dispatched to the front. Despite their skill, they were having a difficult time reducing their speed to perform a proper strafing run on the Polikarpov Po-2 the women flew. The German pilots were also suffering from sleep deprivation as the aerodromes were a favorite target.

On paper, everything was in place. He had assembled a massive force of over one million men and over nine hundred tanks. He was up against a force half its size and not rested. Every day he talked to Chuikov; the general requested more troops to hold his ground. The Germans now controlled ninety percent of the town along with the Mamayev Kurgan—the highest point in Stalingrad. The old Tartar burial ground allowed whoever held it to have a commanding view of all troop movements.

He needed *General Winter* to pick up the pace. Until the Volga froze, there was nothing he could do but keep sending in piecemeal reinforcements to help his comrades.

He paced across the room then sat backdown in his comfortable leather desk chair. The one true high point was the reports concerning the sniper patrols; they were proving extremely effective. Vasily Zaytsev was becoming a national hero. Pravda newspaper made it a point to report his kills every day in hopes it would demoralize the enemy and keep them at bay. He was also pleased with the unofficial reports coming in from a rogue band that was roaming the city. It mentioned how both German and Russian troops were being targeted. He wasn't pleased some of his countrymen were being killed, but he knew it was necessary. Many of the casualties appeared to be from penal battalions or deserters. He shrugged, knowing they would have died either at the hands of the Germans or by firing squad. The door to his office burst open.

"Comrade Zhukov. What news do you have for me today?" bellowed Stalin.

"Comrade Chuikov is holding his ground. Troop buildups continue on the east bank of the Volga. The *Night Witches* continue to harass the enemy. Our sniper teams are performing admirably."

"That is not the news I came to hear."

"Comrade Stalin. Please tell me then what you would like to hear? I have given a concise report on the current battle conditions."

"I want to know when you plan on launching your counterattack and reclaiming my namesake."

"Comrade Stalin. We are waiting for *General Winter* to assist us. When he decides to strike, so shall we."

"And when will that be, Comrade Zhukov?"

"According to the weather reports, within two weeks."

"Two weeks? Two weeks is too long! I want you to strike now. Do you hear me? Now! Our brave men have been fighting heroically for months. They need to be relieved immediately!"

Zhukov poured a cup of tea then took a sip. "Comrade Stalin. To launch now would be foolish. We will have the same results we did in early '42 when you wished to attack the Germans on a broad front when we were not properly prepared. We do not have enough naval vessels or barges to move our troops to the west bank and launch a surprise counteroffensive. It will be a long and laborious process, with the possibility of being detected. This, Comrade Stalin, could result in my well-laid plan failing. Is that what you wish, Comrade?"

Stalin stormed about the room for a few minutes thinking of his options. Zhukov continued drinking his tea, eyeing his leader.

"Comrade Zhukov. You have two weeks. If *General Winter* does not arrive in that time, you are ordered to launch the offensive not later than November 17th. Am I understood?"

He put down his cup. "Yes, Comrade Stalin."

"Good." He walked toward the door. "And Comrade Zhukov?"

He stood up. "Yes, Comrade Stalin."

He smiled. "If you do not attack, you will be sacked." Then he slammed the door shut.

Zhukov walked over to the window and opened it. *If there's a God, hear my words and help me be successful.*

A blast of arctic air blew in his face allowing him to breathe in the cold, harsh, crisp, smell and relax.

*Soon.*

# Chapter 9

# Univermag

**November 12th, 1942**
**Von Paulus Headquarters**

The casualty count kept mounting. Von Paulus was forced to keep pulling units from his right and left flanks. The thought of these areas being defended by the Italians and Rumanians did not allow him much sleep. He could read a map and did not like what he saw. His army was being sucked into a battle they were not experts at. These were not the plains of Poland, Western Europe, or the vast steppes of the Ukraine; this was urban warfare on a scale the academy had never dreamed of. The new army was built to hit fast and hard, and to disorganize the enemy. To date, the tactic of Blitzkrieg had been successful. The capture of over 600,000 Russians in the Kiev pocket filled every soldier with pride. OKW and OKH, along with Hitler, were convinced that no army could sustain such a loss and be able to continue an effective organized resistance. From this day forward, they would be pursuing broken, demoralized units which were only fighting because that fool in the Kremlin did not know when to quit.

For a defeated army, they were taking a horrible toll on his 6th Army as they spent day and night fighting, building by building, block by block, rooting out the stubborn, entrenched Russians. The cost in lives was appalling. The eyes of his men no longer shone. They were black and lifeless. Every day was the same. Capture two blocks, lose one, advance twenty meters, fall back ten. It was maddening. He tried using tanks. They only got in the way or were destroyed by mines or anti-tank rifles. Many of the crews never fired a shot before their carrier was detracked leaving the hulk disabled or burning in flames creating another undesired roadblock

The Luftwaffe had been effective in the beginning, but now they were just bombing empty concrete shells. And, each bomb they dropped seemed to create more hiding places. He hoped he could gain an edge with the addition of Colonel Gough to his force. He knew how demoralizing it was watching men's heads explode from a lone bullet and not being able to find the sniper. Something had to change before his men were too exhausted to carry on.

*And what of this man, Codenamed Otto? Why did Hitler and Himmler insist he be part of the battle? What specialty could he bring that had not already been tried?*

"Excuse me, Herr General."

"What is it, Kurt?"

"Your visitors have arrived."

"Very well, send them in."

Colonel Gough and Otto entered the room. They snapped their heels together. "Heil Hitler."

Gough looked about the room with contempt. It was cramped and dirty just like the men who escorted them in. He was embarrassed at the sight of filthy uniforms and unshaven faces. These were the soldiers of the Third Reich and should look and act like it. He made a note to detail this in his log.

"Heil Hitler. Please be seated." They sat then handed over their orders.

Friedrich glanced them over. "Herr Gough."

"Jawohl, Herr General!"

"Please, let us dispense with the formalities, Colonel. We are not at a dress parade. We are on the front lines."

"Pardon, Herr General, but we are still soldiers of the Third Reich and should act as such."

Von Paulus frowned then looked up. "Colonel, this is Stalingrad. We have no time for such trivial acts you deem not up to your standards. My men and I have been battling for two long months in this city against a very tenacious opponent. Our main goals are as follows:
1) Defeating the Russians
2) Surviving another day
3) Hoping to get one hot meal a day
4) Keeping the lice at bay
5) Bathing once every two weeks

"Any questions?"

"Herr General. I meant no disrespect. I was only trying to bring a semblance of order with me."

He relaxed a little. "Colonel, I appreciate you pointing out the deficiencies of myself and my staff. Trust me. You will soon understand how quickly spit and polish attitudes fade in this environment." He drummed his fingers on his desk for a moment. "However, if you feel you need to make mention of this in your diary, I understand."

A long pause ensued.

"Now, let us discuss your mission. The chemical plant and the surrounding railyard are where you will be hunting. The Russians steal in each night and set mines on the paths we use. We send out sappers each morning to clear them. They usually wind up with a bullet in their head or heart for their trouble. This must stop. They have also been able to set up machine-gun nests in buildings we believe are secure and shoot our men in the back. I do not think I need to explain what type of effect this is having on morale, do I?"

"No, sir."
"Good. Do you have any other questions?"
"Yes, sir. Where is the chemical plant?"
"My aide, Kurt, will fill you in."
"And what about quarters?"

He glanced about his room. "As you can see, accommodations are at a premium. Fear not. We will find something to suit your tastes. Kurt!"

"Jawohl, Herr General."

"Please see if you can find suitable quarters for our esteemed colleague from Berlin. And while you are at it, perhaps our cook can prepare some wiener schnitzel and bratwurst with a mound of sauerkraut."

Gough bristled with the insult. "It is not necessary for you to berate me in front of these men, General. I wish to file a formal complaint immediately on this shabby treatment!"

Von Paulus stood then walked over to Gough. "Herr Colonel, I am trying to prepare you for what you are about to experience, and niceties are not one of them. The papers in Germany speak of great victories and heroic sacrifices. None of that applies to the cauldron you are about to enter. If you still feel the same way in a week, you may file your report. Dismissed."

After Kurt and Gough left, he turned his attention on Otto. "I have been told very little of what your function is to be here. Your orders are just as vague. Would you mind filling me in a little more?"

"Herr General. I am here to hoist our flag in the Central Plaza when the city has fallen and the subhumans are defeated."

He scratched the stubble on his face. "Any man can accomplish that mission. Why you?"

"I am the byproduct of genetic engineering. I am the A-Typical Aryan our Führer has spoken of. He believes the best way to introduce his new race to the world will be when Stalingrad has fallen. No country will stand against us when this glorious victory is secured."

"I see." He rummaged through the orders. "And what do you do until this glorious victory is achieved?"

"I have been ordered to observe and fight when necessary."

"And what training have you had? Infantry? Artillery? Mechanized? Pioneer? Please, do tell me what your specialty is."

Otto stood up, walked towards the desk, raised his right arm, and slammed it down. The oak desk shattered and split in two.

"Herr General. I am trained to kill the enemy no matter what uniform they wear. Any more questions?"

Von Paulus gulped. "None."

"Good. Now let us get down to business, shall we?"

## Chapter 10

## Operation Uranus

### November 14th
### Chuikov's Headquarters

He was bent over his worn, dusty, and torn map. He was running out of men and ammunition. He had received no sizeable reinforcements for a week. Between the Luftwaffe and artillery fire destroying the ferries and docks, passage across the Volga was becoming almost impossible. According to his figures, he was down to fifteen thousand serviceable troops. The other five were being used to bring supplies to the front. Even those stockpiles were dwindling to dangerous levels. His requests to STAVKA were ignored. He knew he and his men had not been forgotten, but why the silence?

"Comrade General. Vasily is here to report."

"Show him in, Yuri."

He limped back to the cave entrance. "The general will see you, Comrade."

"I see you are still healing from your wounds."

"That is none of your concern, Comrade. Please, the general is waiting."

Vasily walked to the desk, saluted and sat. Chuikov did not look up. He finished writing out some orders, reviewed them, then summoned Yuri.

"Send these out immediately."

"Yes, sir. Comrade General."

He pulled out a bottle and poured an ample amount of vodka. He downed it in one swallow.

"And what news do you bring?"

"Comrade General. It has been a successful hunt. Another dozen officers, half-a-dozen machine-gunners, and two dozen runners."

"Yes, that is a successful mission. But I fear it is not enough."

"Excuse me, Comrade General?"

He rose from his chair and began pacing the floor. "I fear STAVKA has forgotten about us. We have received no substantial reinforcements for a week. Even our political commissar, Comrade Khrushchev, is not able to obtain any information. At our present force size, we can hold out for maybe another three weeks. Past that, I do not know."

"Comrade General. I am sure Moscow has its reasons."

"I am sure you are right, but would it harm them to inform us of their plans?"

"I cannot answer that, Comrade."

"Neither can I." He sat back down.

"Comrade General, I have a question."

"Yes."

"Three days ago, there were multiple single shots fired in my sector."

"And? That does not sound unusual."

"Usually not. But these were single shots. One from a Russian rifle, the other from a German. I believe there are other snipers operating in the area."

"You could be correct on the German. We received an unconfirmed report several weeks ago; let me find the communique." He shuffled a few papers. "Here it is. A Colonel Rudolph Gough is being sent here to eliminate the sniper threat. I am guessing they are referring to you."

"Perhaps. I will make him a priority if he is here. And what about the Russian gun?"

Chuikov stared off into the distance. The brooding silence was broken when Yuri and Nikita entered his office.

"General. General. Come quick. The miracle we have been waiting for is arriving."

Chuikov rose from his chair a bit perturbed. "This better be important, Comrades."

Vasily and Chuikov could feel the ground trembling, along with a crushing roar building from the north.

They stood outside the bunker watching the Volga shimmer. He noticed barges were frantically moving to either side of the banks. He looked to the north and what he saw brought a welcome tear to his eyes.

A massive ice floe was pouring down the Volga, crushing everything in its path. Sunken ferries, transports, partial docks disintegrated in its path. Boats trying to cross made haste to the safety of either shore. Some made it; others were crushed and sank.

His warriors on the west and east banks watched in awe as the ice churned south.

His heart filled with relief at the sight. The loss of a few men was nothing compared to what he hoped was about to disrupt the entire 6$^{th}$ Army. For the first time in a long time, he smiled and cheered. *General Winter* had delivered.

He and Nikita yelled out in triumph as the floe sliced its way south. "Now the Germans will feel the wrath of the Red Army!"

Their enthusiasm spread to all the troops. One by one they began shouting and cheering. Many raised their guns and fired into the air. In minutes, the cheering drowned out the sounds of the dying city.

"Soon, we will turn the tables. Nikita, we have much to prepare for."

**Univermag**

"General Paulus. There is activity happening around the Volga."

"What is it, Wilhelm?"

"I am not sure, General. We are getting reports that the Russians are cheering."

"Why would they be cheering? Do they not know we are about to eliminate their last pockets of resistance in a matter of weeks?"

"There are also reports of thunder coming from the north."

"Thunder?" He went outside and looked at the gray, bleak sky. Then he heard it. It was a dull roar that began gaining strength and sound with each passing minute, as that of a Wagnerian opera. The crescendo was getting louder with each passing moment.

"Wilhelm. I want an immediate report from the northern sector. They should be able to see what is going on."

"Jawohl, Herr General."

Von Paulus pulled his gray coat tighter, trying to block out the biting cold. The sound was crescendoing louder and louder. A feeling of dread passed through him.

Wilhelm burst back into the room.

"Well? What did you find out?"

"Ice. It is an ice floe, Herr General."

"What?"

"An ice floe, General. The entire Volga is freezing over."

He turned and looked at Wilhelm, his face blank, the months of fighting etched across his face.

"Wilhelm, I fear our efforts are going to be in vain."

"Herr General. But we are so close to victory."

"We were, Wilhelm. We were. If what you say is true, the Russians can now cross wherever they choose."

He returned to his desk. "If the Volga has frozen, our fate will be determined by the 3rd and 4th Rumanian Armies."

"General?"

"Look at the map, Wilhelm. Up until now, we have been able to strangle the delivery of men and materials to the defenders. They will now be able to choose any area they wish to bring in supplies."

"General. There have been no reports of a Soviet buildup to the east."

"That is true. But then how far has the Luftwaffe reconnoitered out? In the first year of the invasion, we swept across the plains and marshes. We encircled Leningrad and came to within twenty kilometers of the spires of Moscow before they counterattacked. They launched an ill-timed counteroffensive in early '42 with minimal results. When we launched Operation *Blau*, the Soviet forces no longer stood and fought; they withdrew, drawing us deeper and deeper into their country."

"General. The operation has been a success. Our troops have reached the northern slopes of the Caucasus Mountains, we liberated Sevastopol, and now stand on the mighty Volga."

"This is true. But what does it mean?"

"It means the Third Reich will be victorious, Herr General," answered Otto. "I find your attitude and remarks in direct conflict with our Führer's vision. It is men like you who do not deserve to wipe the dirt off our Führer's boots. When our troops have wiped out the Russians, and I have raised our proud flag, I will make sure I mention your subversive attitude in my report."

"Otto, you are free to make that report at any time. In the meantime, I have work to do."

**November 19th**
**7:20am**

Reports began flooding into von Paulus's headquarters. The 3rd Rumanian Army was under attack. He asked for more info. It was not forthcoming. Russian artillery had knocked out communication centers and forward outposts. Instead of dispatching the 16th and 24th Panzer divisions which were heavily engaged in the city, he assigned the 48th to deal with the problem. On paper, they were a formidable force. In reality, they were a worn-out division only capable of slowing down the onslaught, not stopping it. Of the one hundred tanks, many did not have enough fuel or ammunition to stave off a serious Russian attack. Many of their desperately required supplies were lost when the railyard at Kharkov was destroyed.
All they could do was attempt to slow down the juggernaut that was now smashing into the Rumanians.

**November 22nd**
**Kalach**

The unthinkable happened. The Russians trapped and encircled the entire 6th Army. Over 290,000 men and equipment were isolated. Von Paulus made several personal requests to Hitler to allow his worn out, tired men to break out while they still had a chance. Hitler turned him down flat. No German would surrender an inch of soil that so many of his brethren had died and bled over. Goering would make sure his forces received the proper supplies. They were to stand and fight. If a breakout occurred, it would come from a relief army outside the pocket. Von Paulus could do nothing but hope and wait.

**West Bank of the Volga**

Chuikov broke out a new bottle of vodka and two clean glasses. He filled them to the brim.

"Nikita, we have achieved a great victory today. All of our hard work has paid off. Our forces have joined up at Kalach and are expanding the ring around the Germans. Now it will be our turn to show them what it feels like to be cornered."

They toasted each other and downed the hot, burning liquid.

He poured another. "To victory, Comrade."

"To victory, Comrade General."

# Chapter 11

# The Cauldron

**December 10th**
**The Chemical Plant**

"Remember what I taught you, Elizabeth. Breathe slowly as you pull the trigger. Dina, make sure you are ready to take the second shot when the officer comes to verify the kill."

"Yes, Mother."

Each girl exhaled and waited.

The machine-gunner, who had been manning the post for the last three hours, stood to relieve himself. A shot rang out; the bullet pierced his metal helmet. The eyes of the girls were still trained on the post. A minute later, each could see the peaked officer's cap bobbing up and down as he made his way toward the fallen soldier. For a moment, it vanished behind the sandbagged dirt embankment then slowly rose above the barrier. He was panning the gutted buildings with his binoculars trying to locate where the shot came from. A fleck of sunlight struggled through the heavy cloud cover, illuminating a piece of glass. As he turned to call his men, a stream of blood gushed out of his temple.

"Well done, my daughters."

"Thank you, Mother."

Svetlana looked at her warriors, smiling.

"Mother, when can we feed?"

"Tonight."

## General Vasily Chuikov's Headquarters

"Comrade Khrushchev."

"Yes, Comrade."

"How much longer before Zhukov finishes off this pocket?"

"Comrade, I cannot answer that question. I can only report that your men must keep fighting the enemy."

"Comrade! I have no intention of doing otherwise! I only ask so I may plan my own countermeasures. I have been fighting the Germans for the last three months. I have shed more blood of the enemy and my own men than in any other battle. I tire of being on the defensive. I am ready to marshal enough forces to start fighting offensively!"

"Comrade General. Until STAVKA issues those orders, you will continue to keep the front active each and every day. It is your responsibility to make sure no troops are allowed to be withdrawn from the front lines and attempt a breakout. The destruction of the 6th Army will be the largest loss our enemy has suffered, and suffer he must for this unmitigated war he brought to our land. I am sure you agree that this is an important job."

"Yes, Comrade. I agree."

"Good. I have also been informed you will continue to receive reinforcements and ammunition to carry out your orders. Several new batteries of artillery are being dispatched to the east bank to assist in your countermeasures. These units are fresh and ready to rain as much death on our enemy as their barrels will allow."

"They will make an excellent addition."

"I have one other matter to discuss."

"Yes, Comrade."

"What can you tell me of your sniper units?"

"They are performing quite well. Vasily Zaytsev and his units are draining the resolve of our enemy. They are learning the art of hiding."

"Is that all?" inquired Nikita.

"Yes, Comrade."

"I believe you have left out a particular note of interest."

His brow furrowed. He knew what Nikita was asking, but he had taken great pains to omit the rumors he heard from his frontline commanders. He knew they were not rumors but a stark reality that must not surface. He pulled out a stack of papers titled *Unconfirmed*. He leafed through a few of the reports.

"Comrade Khrushchev, if you are referring to the unusual activity surrounding the chemical plant, I can neither deny nor confirm the strange occurrences in that sector."

"But you have units operating there, correct?"

"Yes."

"Then how can you not provide a detailed report?"

"Comrade, it's my job to deal in reality, not fictitious reports."

"Comrade General. It is your sworn duty to inform me of all activities occurring in this city, whether they are confirmed or not!"

Chuikov had done his best to keep the information hidden. The initial reports sent shudders up his spine. Men, both Russian and German, were found completely drained of blood. Some of the bodies revealed two jagged puncture marks in the neck, while others were torn limb from limb with no trace of blood. The reports verified the ferocity of Svetlana and her daughters.

The first report came during a debriefing with Zaytsev. The man was no stranger to death. He had already been credited with over seventy-five kills. Thus, the sight of a dead body should not have unnerved him, but it did. During the review of the day's actions, when he was pressed to describe the bodies and their demise, he could not relay any discernible information. He stared at his commander and uttered one word—vampires. Chuikov immediately issued an order for a two-day rest. He could not have his men worried about such an absurd accusation. Yet he did not dismiss the words of his top sniper. If it was true, which it was, and word spread through his troops that vampires were stalking about the ruins of an already dangerous city, he feared the effect it would have on morale. He sent out various patrols to investigate the matter. None of them returned.

Instead of following the chain of command, he telephoned his supreme commander, Georgy Zhukov, to discuss the troubling matter. Georgy was pleased with the approach as he too understood the ramifications of the story seeping into the troops. All he told him was, "They are old friends. Do not interfere."

"Comrade General. I'm waiting."

"Comrade Khrushchev. As I've already stated, I cannot deny or confirm the activities. If you desire more information, may I suggest you take the matter up with General Zhukov?"

"And why should I take that action?"

"Because, Comrade Khrushchev, to quote our superior, 'They are old friends. Do not interfere.'"

\* \* \*

"Vasily. Where will your unit strike tonight?" inquired Chuikov.

"My units have identified a command bunker approximately two hundred meters from the Kurgan. I believe it's time we paid them a visit."

"Be careful, Comrade."

### 500 meters East of Mamayev Kurgan – 11:00pm

The night sky was filled with angry rolling clouds spitting out snow and ice. The temperature hovered around -10° Celsius. The wind howled out of the north at thirty-five kilometers per hour.

Captain Klein appeared from the wooden reinforced bunker flapping his arms for warmth. He handed a cup of hot ersatz to Corporal Reisen.

"Hans. Are the guards posted?"

"Jawohl, Herr Captain."

"Did your men install all the mines as instructed?"

"Jawohl, Herr Captain."

"Good. I would hate for my sleep to be disrupted tonight."

"Jawohl, Herr Captain."

He turned to enter the secure, warm bunker.

"Hans. Drink your coffee before it freezes. You will be relieved at 2:00am by Johann. If my sleep is interrupted, you'll stand guard duty for the next week. Verstehen?"

"Jawohl."

\* \* \*

### 12:00am

"Andrei, I want you and Fedeya to scout ahead. Look for mines and other booby traps. Get a count on how many guards are posted. Neutralize the mines and traps then come back and report. We will strike when the path is clear."

\* \* \*

"How many do you see, Mother?"

"Enough for a feast."

She watched the sole guard moving back and forth trying to stay warm. She also noticed two other men creeping towards the position.

*   *   *

Andrei and Fedeya slithered through the trench system, taking care to mark mines and disconnect tripwires. Their fingers cracked and bled from the intense cold as they manipulated and defused the deadly weapons and alarm systems. Several times each man had to cup his hands, blowing what minor heat they could summon from their freezing lungs.

With the path clear, they stopped ten meters from the bunker's entrance and watched for guards. After an hour they returned to Vasily, giving a detailed report of the trail they took and the lone guard.

**2:00am**

"Now, girls. It is time to feast."

**2:04am**

"Where is that bastard Johann? He's four minutes late."

A strong gust blew up ice and snow, impairing his vision. He rubbed his eyes, brushing away the frost.

As they refocused, his mind struggled to register what they were seeing. He rubbed them again. Three pairs of green, piercing eyes broke through the darkness.

"Halt. Who are you?" he forced out.

"Your makers!" He lay dead and drained in less than a minute.

"Girls. Shall we see what treasures wait for us inside?"

"Yes, Mother."

Svetlana kicked open the door revealing twenty or so warm bodies. All were asleep with the exception of two. One was getting dressed, while the other was sitting by a small wood stove.

The men stared in horror at the creatures. They noticed blood streaming down the leathery faces of the abominations. One called out with a timid voice. "What and who are you?"

Svetlana flashed her stained teeth, replying in her guttural tone, "Vampires looking for a meal. Appears we have found a feast!"

Before either man could reach for a gun or call out, Dina and Elizabeth flew through the air, latching onto their necks and sucking in the rich, warm, life-sustaining fluid.

Svetlana helped herself to two of the sleeping men.

Dina knocked over a metal canteen, waking Captain Klein.

"Can you idiots not move about in silence?"

"We can," came a raspy response. "But not tonight."

The three commenced to rip apart the remaining sleeping men. The clean, tidy bunker became littered with the remains of the once-proud "Master Race."

She let out a piercing scream. "Now who is the 'Master Race?'"

\* \* \*

Vasily stared at the smashed door. The scream that emanated from the interior of the bunker turned his blood to ice.

"Andrei, I thought you said there was a guard on duty?"

"There was."

"Where is he now?"
"I do not know."
"Did you come across any of our comrades?"
"No."
"Then who is in there?"
"I cannot answer. I would suggest canceling the mission."
"Why?"
"I have a bad feeling."
"So do I." With only two hours of darkness left, if they were going to complete the assignment they would have to act now. They did not want to be caught in no-man's-land when the first rays of sunlight illuminated the battered landscape.
"Andrei. We go now."

\* \* \*

Elizabeth turned her nose to the air. "Mother. I smell fresh blood."
"Yes. We shall eat well tonight."
"Shall we kill them before they enter or wait?"
"We shall wait."

\* \* \*

Vasily and his men burst through the open door, weapons drawn. What greeted them was the most horrendous, gruesome sight they had ever witnessed. The bodies of their sworn enemy were torn and strewn across the room. The stench of bowels assaulted their noses. The dirt walls were covered with blood and intestines. Brain matter squished under their worn boots as they cautiously moved into the room. Two of the men vomited, adding to the horrid smells.
"Vasily. What the hell has happened here?"

"I do not know, Andrei. Someone or something has beaten us here. But what?"

Out of the corner of his eye, he noticed three forms emerging from a dark corner.

His finger froze on his trigger as the aberrations came into the light. The largest one was on him in the blink of an eye, clasping its claws around his neck. The other two figures moved just as fast, disarming the rest of his party.

"Who and what are you?" He forced out.

"Your worst nightmare," came a harsh response.

He took a deep gulp, staring into its fiery green eyes.

"No, you are not. My worst nightmare began a year-and-a-half ago when the Germans invaded my country. And it will continue until my countrymen and I have evicted or killed every last one of them."

The creature's breath penetrated his nostrils, turning his stomach. The sight of skin fragments hanging off her teeth added to his nauseousness.

"You speak bravely for one so close to death."

"I face death every day. The only difference today is, instead of a bullet finding me, it will come from your hands. It will matter not if I live or die today. Death is inevitable for all us."

"Speak for yourself!"

"I am!"

She paused for a moment, circling him. "Do you realize how easy it would be for one of my daughters or me to drain your blood and discard the carcass?"

"From where I stand, yes."

She stopped in front of him. Green fire danced in her pupils. "And that doesn't concern you?"

"No. I have seen more death than any man should witness." She relaxed her grip.

"What is your name?"

"Vasily Zaytsev."

The sound of crackling timber began filling the room. The creature's features began taking on human form. His men were amazed as she transformed.

"Mother!" growled Elizabeth.

"Do it! They are friends."

"NO! They are no better than the Germans." Svetlana spun around, knocking her to the ground.

"Do it now or you will wish you had!"

Vasily and his men stared on in amazement as they turned into beautiful, demure women.

"What are you, if I may be so bold as to ask?" queried Vasily.

"Vampires."

"Why are you in Stalingrad?"

"I was told to come here."

"By whom?"

"That is not your concern."

"Very well. May I ask what your mission is?"

"You may. The same as yours. To rid our country of the Nazis."

"I have heard rumors some of my comrades have met a similar fate. Is this true or speculation?"

"It is true."

"Why do you kill your own?"

"Survival. What we do is no different than what is going on in Leningrad or countless other areas where food is in short supply."

"You realize, as an officer of the Red Army, I'm bound to report this incident?"

"If you feel compelled to tell your superiors of our meeting, let me assure you of one important item—you will die as horribly as those who lie before you. Is that what you wish?"

He surveyed the rotting corpses. "I believe I would prefer a single bullet to the head."

"The choice is yours." He saw glimpses of fire flash across her eyes.

"While you consider the options, think of this. You will be able to report to your superiors of your successful mission tonight and how you eliminated over twenty of the enemy without losing any of your own."

He pondered the thought before proceeding with caution.

"I have one more question before I answer the first. There have been reports of sniper activity around the chemical plant, yet we have dispatched no units to that sector. Could you explain?"

She grabbed his Mosin-Nagant rifle, chambered a round, and pointed it at him. She returned the rifle to him. He looked around the room, confused.

"Question, Vasily?"

"Yes. It's obvious you can kill with stealth, speed, and strength. Why use an ordinary weapon?"

"Sport. Now, have you made a decision concerning your future?"

"Yes. I will make no mention of our encounter in my report."

"A good choice." She looked out the shattered door. The first rays of light were creeping up the horizon. "It's time we all left. Vasily, remember this, my only allegiance is to the survival of my own." She and her girls exited the bunker.

### After-Action Report

Chuikov was hunched over his map as Vasily entered.

"Was it a successful raid, Comrade?"

"Yes."

"How many did you kill?"

He sat down pulling out his worn notebook. "Twenty-five."

"Ranks."

"One major, one captain, two lieutenants, one corporal, and three sergeants. The remaining were privates."

He rubbed his head then clapped his hands together. "Well done, Vasily. With such a loss, I am sure our enemy will think twice about setting up command posts so close to the front."

He hesitated before responding. "Yes, Comrade."

"I detect uncertainty in your voice. Is there something you are not telling me or failed to mention in your report?"

"Nothing of consequence, Comrade."

"I disagree. Your words betray you. What is it, Vasily? What happened which has you troubled?"

He looked at the other men in the dugout. Chuikov instructed them to leave.

"What is it, Vasily? What happened last night?"

"Comrade, I do not know how to tell you this. I gave my word I would not make mention of the events, but as an officer, I feel it my duty to pass on what I witnessed."

"And?"

"Vampires, Comrade. We encountered a group of female vampires last night. They were the ones who destroyed the command post before my men and I struck."

"I see." He scribbled a note on the report then filed it. "You were wise not putting it in the report. They are our allies. Make sure your men speak nothing of the events. They are personal friends of General Zhukov. It would displease him if we exposed their existence. Understood?"

"Yes, Comrade."

"Good. Then let us drink to our combined victory and those we shall achieve!"

He called all the men back into the dugout.

"Gentlemen, fill your glasses to the brim. We are in the presence of a hero. His men disposed of twenty-five of our enemy last night, and I'm putting him up for the Order of Lenin!" The men shouted in unison.

"To Vasily Zaytsev! Hero of the Soviet Union!"

Vasily raised his glass with trepidation.

\*\*\*

### December 25th

Von Paulus stared at his shrinking defensive perimeter. His last ray of hope faded when the relief offensive, *Wintergewitter,* stalled. His men on the southern and western trenches could see and hear the battle as General Hoth moved to within twenty kilometers of the encircled army. He wanted to assist in the escape but could not. The supplies Goering promised never appeared. He promised Hitler his Luftwaffe would have no problem supplying his fellow Germans. Like his boasts about destroying the BEF at Dunkirk, he failed. The planes that did land could not deliver the minimum requirements of food per man. What the brave pilots were able to do was evacuate as many troops as they could at great peril to themselves.

Von Paulus scanned across the last open airport. The runway was littered with wrecked Ju 88's and 52's. Through the strong north winds, he could still hear and smell the wounded and dying lying around the airstrip, hoping to be delivered from the nightmare. He shook his head in disgust.

He walked amongst the men, attempting to give them hope and encouragement. A few of the men he spoke with were stirred with his words. They still believed in the cause. Many only stared at him into nothingness. There was a hint of hope in their eyes, but that too would extinguish if help did not arrive soon.

He walked back to his staff car with a steady but even gait. He desperately tried to shake off the cold and the stench of rot, hopelessness, and death from his overcoat. "Take me back to headquarters."

He placed one more call to OKH wanting to know when his men would be saved. The answer was the same as the last time he called.

"Hold on. We are coming," replied Keitel.
"When?"
"When appropriate forces are gathered."
"When will that be?"
"When we are ready. Until that time, continue to fight. Heil Hitler."
The line went dead.

## Chapter 12

## Sniping

**Chemical Plant - one week later**
**Thirty minutes before dawn**

It did not take Rudolph long to understand what von Paulus warned him about. Stalingrad was the most miserable city he ever visited. It was nothing like The Hague, Paris, Sedan, or even Krakow. The town was nothing more than a burnt-out hulk. His palate was getting used to the daily dose of horse meat. Never in his life had he ever thought of killing a horse for food. Here, it was a necessity—horse meat or rat. And then there was the ever-present presence of the most hated vermin in this city—lice. They were everywhere. He did what everyone else learned to do, live with them; they were not going anywhere.

He pulled out his logbook and smiled. In one week, he had taken out five officers and two machine-gunners. He thought that when he presented his report, the general would be impressed. Instead, von Paulus only grumbled. They had lost twice that many in half the time. He was told that it was time to stop shooting for sport and get down to business. He needed the Russian snipers caught or killed. He did not care which. Until he accomplished that, he need not come back to headquarters and report.

He pulled his scarf tighter around his neck to fight off the constant cold. *I will show von Paulus my worth. The sooner I find and kill my enemy, the sooner I leave and return to civilization.*

He looked through his scope searching for the vermin he knew were scurrying about preparing their morning sortie to harass his countrymen. There, movement to the right.

One, two…no…more Schmidt bobbing flat helmets. He moved his rifle to the right. Fifty meters from the approaching squad was a group of Germans smoking. By the dirt and grime and weary looks on their faces, they had just returned from a night patrol. Since he had no radio to alert them, he contemplated firing a shot to awaken them from their numbness. If he did shoot, they would take cover and look in the wrong direction. It would be necessary to line up on the first target that popped over the wall or in the open, in hopes his comrades would come out of their comatose state.

He moved the rifle back to the left. *Where are they? Where did they go?* As the sun broke over the horizon, the cold, unrelenting wind picked up, sprinkling dust and dirt from the hole in the floor above him. He wiped the dirt from his face and his eyepiece. He took a deep breath, then peered through the scope again. *There they are.* Only twenty meters from the squad, but not exposed enough to get off a kill shot.

There was an open alley about six meters wide that separated the two forces. The clang of metal caught his attention. A sergeant was bringing the men breakfast. It amazed him how a town filled with so much death could be so quiet.

He moved his scope back to the Russians. They disappeared again. That meant they were at the wall adjacent to the alley. His first shot must be true. If not a kill, then a piercing wound which would have the victim screaming.

The first helmet popped out then back. They were preparing to move. He took another deep breath and exhaled. The helmet appeared again for a few more seconds. He waited. It would only be a few more seconds before they charged. *Eins, Zwei, Drei,* Fire!

The victim slumped to the ground holding his chest, screaming. Instead of coming to his aid, his comrades rushed past him with machine guns blazing. They were met with a hail of gunfire and crumpled to the ground. He smiled knowing his job was done. He wondered if his comrades knew or cared how close they were to dying. He opened his logbook and decided not to record the encounter. Von Paulus wanted dead snipers filling his pages, not inconsequential soldiers.

As he closed the book, he heard another shot ring out from the south. It was close. He looked through his scope scanning the group he had saved. The sergeant who brought the morning rations was lying on his side, dead. His comrades had taken cover. He left his cover and moved to the south side of the building.

He found a hole the size of a small kitchen chair in the wall. He moved a few pieces of broken furniture for concealment. He lay down and started scanning the other buildings in the square.

"Where did it come from? Where would I take up position to make such an excellent shot? Where are you my freund? Show yourself so I may send you to the underworld. Do not be shy. I will be merciful with one bullet."

He kept looking and watching. Sooner or later they would show themselves.

\* \* \*

"That was an excellent shot, Elizabeth. Dina, it is now your turn. Do exactly as your sister did. Pick a stick, take a deep breath, then pull the trigger slowly."

"Mother, I know what I am doing. I do not need you constantly telling me what to do."

"Make sure you keep the rifle out of the window and hidden. The sun is starting to rise and could give us away."

Svetlana watched each and every building in the vicinity. She knew they were not alone. Hopefully, Elizabeth's shot would force his hand. She kept looking.

"Mother. They are not showing themselves. I say we move to another location where we have a more advantageous position."

"We are fine where we are. Show patience and we will be rewarded."

She did not notice Dina edging closer to the opening in the wall. The sun's rays started creeping into the hideout.

"Hello, Liebchen," whispered Gough.

Svetlana noticed a wisp of dust filter out from a hole in the building three hundred meters away and then saw the small metal cylinder and a puff of smoke.

"Dina! MOVE!"

\* \* \*

Vasily was taking a bite from his rationed hard black bread when the second shot rang out. He picked up his binoculars trying to figure out where the shots were coming from. The sounds came from the bombed-out chemical plant. He spent five minutes panning building after building, floor after floor with no result. One shot was German and one Russian. He now knew he was not alone. But who were they? On his last report to Chuikov, there was no mention of other sniper squads operating in his sector. He would address the issue again when he reported in three days. For the moment, he would need to be extra careful.

He leaned back against the wall, blocking off the piercing wind, reviewed his logbook, took another bite of bread, placed it in his rucksack, and nodded off.

# Chapter 13

# Rostov-on-Don

### Five miles Southeast of Bataysk – 10:00pm

Over the past few weeks, Konstantin allowed Roman to plan the entire raid. He wanted to make sure the boy, now becoming a man, was capable in all areas of military planning: scouting, recording, plotting, analyzing, and formulating. If he proved his talents were blossoming, Konstantin knew he would make an excellent lieutenant in the future.

\* \* \*

"Are you positive about the size of the garrison?" asked Konstantin.

Roman ran his hands across the parchment he had prepared. "Yes. From six in the morning till eleven o'clock, the battalion is drilling. Eleven to twelve, they go to the mess hall. Twelve to two, they practice parade formations. Two to six, the crews and mechanics go over the machines and repair any problems they encounter. At six, they head to the mess tent leaving exactly forty men walking the grounds. At seven, the guard changes so that those who stood watch can fill their bellies. At nine, a fresh guard of twenty take their place. These guards have shown a lackluster interest in their duty. They spend the next three hours smoking cigarettes, drinking, playing cards, or lying by the vehicles, daydreaming or sleeping. At 11:30pm, the officer on watch makes his inspection tour ensuring everyone is awake and at their posts."

"Why?"

"The camp major and colonel perform a surprise visit between midnight and 2:00am. Those found not at their posts are dealt with harshly."

"How?"

"One night, two of the guards were accused of abandoning their posts. They were shot on sight. Another night, a guard was found in one of the vehicles with a local whore. The next day, he was tied to the undercarriage of a tank and dragged around the parade ground for over an hour."

"Did he survive?"

Roman looked up. "Does it matter?"

"No." He let out a suppressed chuckle. "What do you think of these disciplinary actions?"

"I believe they are quite fitting for the crime." He paused for a moment. "Do you not agree?"

"Roman, I would not have been so lenient, but yes, the punishment is appropriate." He moved around the table. "Anything else I should know?"

"Occasionally, the crews will come out to check their machines between two and four."

"Why? That seems peculiar since they will be drilling again in the morning."

"That, I cannot answer. Perhaps they are bored and restless waiting to go into battle. Perhaps they do not trust the guards to perform their duties, or maybe they have a sense of emptiness when they are not around their vehicles."

"Interesting." He paced about the room thinking then returned to the table, re-examining the map. "Based on the information you have at hand, what time do you propose we strike?"

Roman fired off with authority. "Two-thirty in the morning."

"Why?"

Roman glared at Konstantin. He was tiring of being questioned. "Uncle, you are trying my patience. I have scouted the camp for the last two weeks and know every move and guard the Germans have. I am so familiar with their routine I could walk across the compound and they would never know I was there. Furthermore—"

Konstantin reached over the table, grabbed Roman's tunic, and dragged him across the table. "Because I want to know and that is all you need to know. You are still a private in my army and will act as one. Do you think I would send this clan off into the dark without being armed with a complete report on the target?" He shook him hard. "Do you, boy?"

Roman was not fazed. He knew he was right and was not going to back down. He grabbed his uncle's hand, wrenching it free. Regaining his footing he straightened out his tunic.

"I am no longer a boy, Uncle!" He straightened up his ruffled blouse. "Perhaps a year ago, your assessment would have been correct. Today, it is not. I am more of a man than my father and your brother, Nikoli. I have studied and learned how to lead patrols and plan attacks with minimal losses. If you do not trust me, then you should have performed the task yourself!"

He let out a laugh that shook the timbers in the roof. The outburst brought Irina, Kirilli, Kladviya, and Boris running into the room.

"What is so funny?' demanded Irina.

"Yes, tell us now so we can enjoy the joke," chimed in Kirilli.

He wiped tears from his soaked cheeks. "It appears my young protégé has grown a pair and become a man. Kirilli, you should be proud of this boy. No…excuse me…man. He has been describing how we are going to attack the German compound and with great panache. He also, in so many words, informed me I was full of shit. Can you believe that? A Boirarsky standing up to a Romanov and telling him he is full of shit?"

All but Kirilli found the moment amusing.

"Son. Did you actually tell him that?"

"In so many words, yes Father, I did."

"Have I not cautioned you about such language? We win our battles with—"

"Hard words of war, Father? Unlike your plan, mine will not fail. There will be no losses to our own, only the enemy. My plan is flawless, and you would do well to listen and learn."

The air became silent and still. Father and son were locked in a major stare down.

"Gentlemen. Gentlemen," interjected Konstantin. "We have enough problems without turning on ourselves. Kirilli, Roman is no longer a boy. What he has told me so far is an excellent, well-thought-out plan. We were about to discuss the time of the attack when he and I had our own disagreement. I suggest we all stand back and let him finish. Roman, the floor is yours again."

The others circled around the table taking in the details of the map.

"As I was saying, we will attack at 2:30am."

"Why do you think 2:30 is the ideal time?" Konstantin asked again.

Roman looked up and smiled. "It is a calculated risk. We will capture one, two, or even three crews."

"How can you be sure of this coup?" asked his father.

"Because I have reconnoitered the site and noted their daily tendencies. Now, if you do not mind, I will explain our battle plan."

"I am not convinced of your—"

"Then stay behind, Father. There is no room for doubt in what we are about to embark upon. Are you with us or not?"

All eyes turned on him.

Kirilli took a step back then bowed his head, glancing at the map. "Proceed, son."

**2:00am**
**Headquarters-Bataysk**

"Major Kruger. Are the guards posted?"
"Jawohl, Herr General."
"When was the last time you checked on them?"
"Two hours ago, Herr General."
"Was all in place?"
"Jawohl, Herr General."
"Good. Good." He paused for a moment. "It is imperative that we keep our men on a razor-sharp edge. I have information that our forces will soon be going into action."

"Do you know where, Herr General?"
"It is up to the Führer, but it looks like we will be marching to the northeast. Von Paulus is having a tough time reaching the Volga. The Russian defense has stiffened with each meter he advances. Of course, he is handicapped with the Rumanian and Italian divisions driving on his flanks. They are hardly frontline forces and are better relegated to being behind the front lines handling supply, prisoners, and security. However, since the majority of our top divisions are engaged or recuperating, we are forced to deal with what is available at the moment." He paused, looking out the window taking in the view of his formidable panzer force. "Kruger."

"Yes, Herr General."
"Have you heard any more of partisan activities in this area?"
"Nein, Herr General."
"Gut. Das ist gut. Keep your ears open. I have received several communiqués from OKH on increased activities at our rear. It would not do well if any of our units were sabotaged on the eve of our pending victory, Major."

"Agreed, Herr General."

"Let us make one more round of the compound before turning in."

"Jawohl, Herr General."

**2:20am**
**One hundred meters South of Bataysk**

Roman glanced at his watch again.

"Nervous?"

He gave Konstantin a quick look. "Not at all. The plan is solid. Only anxious to put it into action."

"Patience, Roman. You have planned it well and everyone is in place."

They both scanned the compound. Roman perked up when he saw two officers making the expected round.

"Uncle. Appears this will be more profitable than I first envisioned."

"Why?"

"See the tall officer?"

"Yes."

"I have only seen him once. He is the commanding general of the battalion. I believe his name is Guttenberg."

"This is important why?"

"Who better able to train us in the operation of the tanks than him?"

"Excellent idea. We need to inform the others so they do not kill him outright." A smile crept up Konstantin's lips.

"Agreed. I will go and—"

"No. I will warn them. You keep an eye on him and make him your priority. The others and I will implement the rest of the plan. And Roman, good luck."

**2:29am**

General Guttenberg and Major Kruger were finishing the surprise inspection. All seemed in order.

"Major Hofstetter, I am pleased with what I have seen. The men and machines appear in order. You have done well in preparing them for the upcoming battle. I will be leaving tomorrow for Kharkov where I will receive my final orders. As soon as I know what direction we are headed you will be informed.

"Danke, Herr General. Can I offer you an ersatz or something stronger before turning in?"

"I think something stronger is in order as we prepare to begin the final assault of eradicating the Bolshevik menace."

"Agreed, Herr General."

Both men started walking towards the major's office. The general stopped in his tracks and tilted his head to the right.

"Major. Did you hear something?"

"Nein, Herr General. Shall we go in?"

"Wait a moment." They stood silent. The sound of tree limbs cracking carried across the yard.

"There. Did you hear it that time?"

"Yes. But it is nothing to worry about. Probably some animals rustling out in the fields, sir."

"Yes, that would be the case if there were woods in the area, but there are not."

A high-pitched ear-splitting cry broke the silence and their thoughts.

"MEIN GOTT!"

**2:30am**

Roman wasted no time disposing of Kruger. With one swipe of his claw, Kruger's head flew off his shoulders then bounded down the hard-packed road. Guttenberg reached for his Luger too late. The same clawed hand grabbed him, breaking bones, and bending the butt of the pistol.

The creature's eyes burned with a purplish fire. The stench of death radiated from its breath as its face closed the distance between the two.

The proud German did his best to retain his composure and not cry out like a little schoolgirl as he gripped his busted hand. Fighting back the pain, he tried to stand up to the creature.

"I am…General Guttenberg. Commander…of the Fourth…Panzer Army. I should warn you…your actions…will lead…to your death. We have ways—"

His tirade was cut short as Roman wrapped his claws around his throat then revealed his two-centimeter fangs. Guttenberg did his best to break the vice grip with his one good hand and failed. The creature pulled him close to his face until the two were nose to nose.

Through a guttural, scratchy sound he made out the words, "Live or die."

As his mind wrapped around the ultimatum, the sounds of his guards dying filled his ears. He chose the only wise option open. "Live."

Roman dropped him to the ground, kicked him in the ribs, breaking two of them, then snarled. "Stay!" Then vanished into the night.

The operation's success surprised even Konstantin. The number of guards was exactly as Roman had described. Those who were not dispatched or fed on were converted for training purposes.

When the bloodshed was over, one by one the members returned to their human form.

Roman watched Guttenberg struggling to crawl to his office to sound the alarm.

"Herr General. While I commend your efforts, they are in vain. You chose to live, remember? Thus, it is time to grant your wish, although not as you might think."

He bent over, placed his incisors over the veins, dug deep, and began to feed.

He relished the smell of the rich copper fluid coursing through his body. The general was of good stock. Such a pity he could not share with the others.

\* \* \*

Konstantin surveyed the yard. The clans and their consorts milled about.

"Roman, what is our next move?"

He wiped the blood from his face. "When the general returns to our world, he will give the orders to his men to mount up. We can either walk or ride with them. I would suggest riding as our people need to start familiarizing themselves with the tanks.

"An excellent suggestion, Roman. Excellent suggestion."

When General Guttenberg came to, he gave the correct orders under the eyes of Roman and Konstantin.

They each boarded a tank, placing themselves in the commanders' cupola and headed home.

\* \* \*

**Two Days Later**

Von Manstein stood in silence at the carnage that lay before him. The icy wind cut through his greatcoat as he inspected the compound. Partisans had not only attacked the training grounds at Bataysk; there were no survivors. And over twenty of his precious tank reserves were gone. Those still remaining were gutted. It would take at least a month to bring them back to service. He needed those tanks to break through the iron circle the Russians had built up around von Paulus and the encircled 6th Army. Without them, his chances of success dropped at least twenty percent.

Even though the SS had sealed the camp off, how could he explain the deaths of over a hundred men and the fifty that were missing? The bodies that were found or the pieces of them could not be sent home. There was no way to make sure what parts went where as they were mangled beyond recognition. Many of the ID tags were also missing. He smiled knowing the grisly details of disposal were in the hands of the SS. He was adamant with the officer in charge not to notify his superiors, and that his report would go through his headquarters for final approval before being sent to Berlin.

He would have to tell the Führer of this unfortunate raid, or he could wait until after the breakout was successful. Hitler would be angry at first, but would then hopefully shake it off and attribute it to the perils of warfare. He dismissed the thought after contemplating it. Best to get it over with now. He walked into Gutenberg's office.

He was pleased how orderly it remained after the attack. No noticeable sign of struggle which suited him. He did not wish to make the call in an office that had been ransacked or covered in blood. He sat down, picked up the phone, and asked to be connected to OKH and the Führer. A bead of sweat navigated down his nose.

\* \* \*

"Are you aware of what your incompetence has cost us?" railed Hitler at Himmler.

"The hopes of the 6th Army are most assuredly in jeopardy because your security forces have not been able to protect our vital supplies and equipment! I stand on the precipice of freeing the world from the mongrel hordes and restoring the Aryan Race as masters of all Europe and Eastern Europe. I will not be denied my destiny! Do you hear me? I will not be stopped from fulfilling what the Gods have foretold me. We are only months away from achieving my goals. Do you hear me? Only months and now this. What have you to say for yourself?

Himmler adjusted himself in the leather chair. "Mein Führer. This is but a minor setback. Von Manstein has sufficient forces to carry out his duties. Do not worry. He will be successful. You know how generals are. Much too cautious at times."

Hitler sat down and took a breath. "You are right. I should not let minor issues cloud my vision. Still, the attack should have never occurred and been so successful."

"I agree. I have already made the appropriate measures to beef up security and punish those who failed us."

"Good. Good."

"And remember, we have Otto in Stalingrad. He will not fail."

"Yes, I had forgotten that fact. Thank you for reminding me."

Himmler glanced at the clock on the wall. "The hour is getting late. Have you dined yet?"

"After receiving the news, I had lost track of time. You are correct; let us go eat. You can fill me in on how Otto is performing."

How could he inform him of Otto's activities? He hoped his comment would deflect any more inquisitions about him. He had heard nothing from von Paulus for over two weeks on the topic. He would do his best to steer away from the subject during their dinner. Adolph did not need any more bad news.

# Chapter 14

# Thoughts

Vasily was not pleased with his kill count the last few weeks. While he knew his countrymen had struck a devastating blow to the enemy, their success was interfering with his work. The Germans were no longer launching local attacks. They were hunkered down and waiting for the siege to be lifted. He was forced to operate much closer to the enemy than was advisable. He considered 500 meters a safe distance before the attack. Now, he was having to work to within 150 meters of his prey. His real worry was the enemy he had yet to see.

\* \* \*

Rudolph was in a situation he was not used to—helplessness. He was a man who prided himself on being in control. It was the way he lived his life. In school, he excelled in academics, many times showing up his professors. When they revolted by punishing him, he would study harder to make sure his arguments were impenetrable.

One day, he was in a heated debate with his physics teacher on the probability of breaching the sound barrier with an engine yet to be developed. The debate wound up in the headmaster's room. The headmaster listened to both sides before excusing them from the room. Ten minutes later, they were summoned back in. There were at least six books on theoretical physics spread out before them. Rudolph won. He graduated first in his class.

In officer's school, it was no different. At an astonishing rate, he absorbed all the tactics he found useful:

Bismarck, Ludendorff, Napoleon, Stonewall Jackson, Grant, and Lee. He could dissect a battlefield and propose an effective countermeasure. This did not always please his instructors, but they realized when they were bested.

But this—this was different. The entire 6th Army was surrounded and cut off with a standing order to hold. Hold what? A bombed-out hulk? And for what? He amazed himself how cynical he had become. He now understood the commanding general's tone when they first met; von Paulus had spoken the truth without sounding treasonous.

Before his arrival, he believed everything the papers printed. They all stated that victory was only weeks away. Soon, the Russians would beg for mercy and come flooding to the German lines with their hands raised ready to join up and defeat Stalin and his henchmen. Reality was more sobering than the false truths being printed. He now realized many of the photos showing Russian women welcoming, hugging, and kissing his comrades were staged. No such places or people were in this city and probably never were.

The weather was the worst he could imagine. The thermometer hovered around -10 to 0 degrees Celsius. He pulled his wool scarf tighter trying to fend off the incessant cold. It reminded him of his deer hunt so many years ago. He thought he would never be that cold again; he was wrong. There was no room to escape to and relax by a blazing fire with a brandy snifter. There was no chance of a change of clothes, but the worst part was relieving oneself. Urination was tricky but manageable. Evacuating the bowels was a whole different story. Many were dying because their rectums were freezing solid. "GOD. How did I wind up here?"

His concern was no longer filling his logbook up with kills—it was surviving.

\* \* \*

Von Paulus stared at the current order from OKH.

*General von Paulus,*

*You are to hold your position and wait for help.*

*Signed,*
*General Wilhelm Keitel*

He looked up from the paper.
"With what, Kurt? With what?"
"Excuse me, Herr General?"
"Nothing. I was talking out loud."
He looked at his watch—5:00pm. He cringed knowing what was next.
Otto moved to the radio. "Herr General. It is time to listen to Radio Berlin for today's inspirational words from Goebbels."
The radio crackled as it warmed up.

*Guten Tag meine Freunde*

*I bring great news to the German people today. Our glorious forces in Stalingrad have dealt the enemy a heavy defeat. Over five hundred tanks, one hundred planes, and countless caches of weapons were destroyed this week. Over ten thousand of the enemy have been killed, along with another ten thousand surrendered or were absorbed into our mighty forces.*

*General von Paulus assures our Führer he will defeat the forces surrounding him; he will break out and destroy all Russian filth in his vicinity. It is only a matter of time.*

*People of Germany, we must honor our warriors who have been ordained by God and the Führer to rid the world of Communism and Jewry. To obtain these goals, we at home must suffer more depravations. While our bellies grow fat, those of our men are empty. While we can wrap ourselves in warmth with clothing and fire, our men are in tatters with only small kerosene lamps for heat.*

*Once again, we are asking for our strong people to give all you can and more to help our glorious men achieve the victory we all seek and deserve. The more we suffer at home, the stronger our soldiers resolve will be.*

*Heil Hitler!*

"Perhaps Herr Goebbels should actually come and visit us before making such outlandish statements."

"General, I tire of your defeatist talk. I have already informed my superiors of your attitude."

Von Paulus stared a hole in Otto. "How blind are you, man? Look around you? Do you see schnitzel and strudel filling our tables? Do you see potatoes and beets in our warehouses? Are our cooks overburdened with sausages and cattle to feed the troops? And what of this great offensive we launched? When was it, and where was I when we crushed the Russians?" He glanced to his left. "Kurt, do you remember me issuing the order to attack? "

"General, I will hear no—"

"Whether you want to believe it or not, you will listen. If a breakout attempt is not organized soon, I fear you will not be performing your important mission. However, if you still believe our situation is salvageable, please, tell me." He took a breath. "In fact, tell us all what to do."

He walked up to von Paulus, slapping him hard. "Your insolence will not go unpunished. When we are victorious here, I promise to be your hangman at the court-martial."

Von Paulus rubbed his jaw. He was relieved to find out it was not broken. "Until that time, Major, you are ordered to leave my headquarters and not to return until you are prepared to formerly apologize for your actions and make amends."

"Where do you propose I go?"

"I do not care. Perhaps you can find the magical force that is going to free us from our current situation. Now, get out."

\* \* \*

## Moscow

"Comrade General. Let me be the first to congratulate you on a superb offensive. Even though I believe you should have struck sooner, I cannot argue with success."

"Thank you, Comrade Stalin. Let me remind you that a caged animal is a dangerous creature. When they realize there is no hope of escape, they become unpredictable and will fight to the death."

Stalin let out a hearty laugh. "True, General. But if the creature has no teeth, it is nothing more than noise. A toast to our victory."

Georgy picked up his glass. "To the Motherland and victory."

"The Motherland and victory!"

They clicked the glasses and swallowed their vodka.

\* \* \*

Svetlana wiped away the plaster from Elizabeth's forehead. The bullet only grazed her. Dina was beside herself for a few days fearing she was almost responsible for her sister's death. She would be more careful and listen to her mother from now on when it came to a tactical situation.

"Mother."

"Yes, Dina."

"When are we going to feed? It has been over three days since our last meal."

"Yes, it has. Elizabeth is still too weak to move. I will go out tonight and see what I can find."

"Where have the Germans gone?"

"I do not know. I can only guess that since the river froze, a major battle took place and the Germans lost."

"Can you be sure?"

"No. I can only guess, and for now, that should be enough. I will leave tonight and hopefully bring back a body or two. I am also thinking about changing our tactics. Picking off a few sticks each day is becoming tiresome. I think we should consider another attack on an outpost."

"German or Russian?"

"Does it matter?"

A blast of cold air whipped through the room when she opened the broken door.

\* \* \*

Otto paced and fumed in front of the Univermag cursing von Paulus and his arrogance. *How dare he suggest they were losing the war. How dare he belittle the words of Goebbels and Hitler.* He looked up at a bent streetlight and envisioned von Paulus's body swaying from it at the end of a rope.

He shivered as a blast of cold air roared down the street. There was something different in the air. A scent he had never encountered before—a female, almost like him.

His body began contorting. The guards patrolling the front of the building became nervous with the sounds he was making.

*This is what Himmler and Dr. Brandt had been talking about.* He held his hands before his face, watching blood seep from the nail beds as the nails grew into long, sharp talons. He moved his neck side to side as his jaw shifted for the feeding teeth. He could feel muscle and sinew snapping and growing with each second that passed.

The guards unslung their weapons, barking undecipherable orders.

He glared back at them and snarled. His size and strength had tripled in only minutes. He took in a deep breath of the ice-cold air; it invigorated his body

He heard shots, then felt needles pinch his skin. The guards were firing on him. Wasting no time, he lunged at them. They were too startled to keep firing. They stopped when Otto grabbed their heads in each hand and bashed them together.

He turned towards the street letting out a piercing howl, then ran off.

\* \* \*

Elizabeth jerked up from her sleep. "Mother, something is coming."

*A creature like me?*

# Chapter 15

# Otto

He cared not for the men he so readily disposed of at Univermag—they were but humans. Von Paulus knew nothing of his mission or his genetically altered physique. He was the embodiment of the master race his Führer kept pounding into the populace. The German people were destined to rule the world, and men like him were the answer. His type was impervious to pain and held remarkable healing powers which many a doctor would envy.

Physically, he was a daunting two-a-half meters tall and one hundred kilograms. Goebbels had his propaganda machine in full force, parading his picture in all the papers proclaiming Otto was the Nordic God they were all descendants from. He wanted to interview him and have him travel the country, showing off this magnificent specimen of German ancestry and superiority. Himmler told him point-blank, no, and Hitler backed up the decision. They agreed he could use him as only a tool of propaganda. His existence and mission were to remain secret. Once he accomplished his assigned task, the whole world would know of his presence, and that resisting the Third Reich would be pointless.

He laughed to himself when he was able to start cataloging and retaining knowledge: Hitler—a hysterically unstable madman who never knew when to shut up. Himmler—a weasel of a man with the intellect of a small snail. He would be better suited as a shopkeeper, accountant, or a poor chicken farmer. Goebbels—a dwarfy, club-footed imbecile. The man could talk for hours and say absolutely nothing of value. And yet, they referred to themselves as the master race. Master race indeed! He was what they all strived to be. He was the wave of the future, and his future plans had nothing to do with the mission they sent him off to complete.

He could care less about raising a flag in Red Square. His goals were loftier and of much more importance. His…quote…masters might be able to affect his physical attributes, but they did not, nor could they, control his thoughts.

He vaguely remembered his human parents and their willingness to allow Hitler and his henchmen to recruit him and experiment on him. He never outwardly showed pain during the horrendous experiments they conducted on him. Each time he received a new injection, he turned his thoughts to visiting his parents one day and repaying them for the unrelenting pain and suffering he had been forced to endure against his will. He learned to manage the pain, but he could not manage his dreams. It was the only thing that scared him.

Images of white fangs, green, red, and blue orbs of light flashed through his mind. The screams of people and animals dying rang through the darkness. Garbled, hissing voices pierced his ears. At first, he did not understand who or what they were, but as time wore on, he began to feel a strong connection to these creatures that filled his thoughts.

They were giants among men. They lived for centuries. They defeated and destroyed those who stood in their way. They had had their share of defeats against a few foes, but their greatest enemy was their own kind. Their fights were violent and unrelenting. They never took prisoners unless, it appeared to him, it would be best for the collective. But who were they and where did they reside?

The scent he detected earlier became stronger as he weaved his way north, through the ruins of what was once a thriving metropolitan city. He could sense eyes upon him and ignored them. They were not important unless he decided to feed. He reveled and scoffed at the destruction man had created. Who caused it was unimportant. He knew through his teachings this was what man did best—build, destroy, then build again. What a futile existence humankind created for themselves. To him, it was pointless.

His kind, whatever they were, were more than capable of exterminating mankind and its high regard for itself. They were nothing more than a source of food and enjoyment. Forms to be played with then dispensed of when they no longer served a purpose. That was his mission. He knew through Hitler and Himmler they were only focused on the Jewish race and its annihilation. He would see to it that plan was expanded for the entire human race. That put a smile on his face.

A yell interrupted his pleasing thoughts.

"Halt. Or I'll fire."

He panned the bombed-out shells of the buildings surrounding him.

"Komm here."

He saw the man rising from the rubble of concrete and steel. The soldier appeared to be in his late twenties, early thirties. The soft visor cap told him he was an officer. His uniform was grimy and dusty. His eyes detected, with excellent clarity, the Wound Badge, Iron Cross First Class, Second Class ribbon, and the Knight's Cross hanging from his neck. Perhaps he will be a worthy opponent though highly unlikely. The officer's tone was indignant and arrogant. Otto detected a bit of hesitancy with his last command. The longer he did not respond the more unsure the officer became. He glanced back and forth giving out commands to his unseen forces and then began walking towards Otto.

"Wie ist Ihr name?"

He let the man move closer, scanning the area the officer came from. Several steel helmets were seen moving about. He heard the clicking of a cartridge being loaded, and began moving towards the officer. He also detected restless movement in some of the other buildings; they reminded him of rats looking for food. *They should have remained cowering in their holes.*

The officer's eyes were glued on Otto as the distance closed and he began reaching for the Luger in its holster. The leather strap was stuck. When the officer looked down to fix the problem, Otto lunged forward striking the officer, carrying them both into the dugout, and crashing into the rest of the squad. Not a sound was heard as he dispatched all four men.

The sound of rifles and machine pistols filled his ears. Dust and concrete flew round him as the infuriated soldiers shot at him. He moved into the interior of the building identified a stairwell and moved to the third floor in seconds. He peered across the road locating where the fire was coming from; he leaped the thirty feet separating the buildings landing on the roof in seconds, he descended the stairs, coming up behind the men looking for him.

"Comrades?"

They were stunned he was behind them and were never given a chance to protest the situation as his talons ripped through their throats sending them to the promised land.

He drank what he required, then for his personal fun and amusement, dismembered each body with a surgeon's precision. He then took the parts and decorated the building as a warning to those who might stand in his way.

He walked out into the street. The sun was setting as eerie shadows descended on the war-strewn landscape.

The icy wind whipped up wisps of snow. It also carried a scent he was following. He let out a loud piercing howl and moved towards the smell. He was getting closer to what he believed was one of his own.

# Chapter 16

# Hunting Grounds

**December 30th**

Von Paulus stared at the map with great consternation. The black lines depicting the position of the Russian forces were inexplicably squeezing his defensive perimeter smaller and smaller. He was plagued with second-guessing his decision of waiting on General Hoth's relief effort. Despite Hitler giving him a direct order not to assist in the relief effort, it would have been better to fight than to sit and wait. To disobey his Führer could have led to a demotion and possible court-martial. It would have brought disgrace to himself and his family. Contemplating the current predicament of his once-proud army, the risks definitely outweighed the consequences he now faced. His men would be saved. They would be able to rest, regroup, rearm, and then join other units in order to thwart the Russian counteroffensive, and restabilize the front line putting them in a good position to regain the lost ground. He rose from his chair and began pacing the room.

He scoffed at his past decisions and what actions he should have taken. A child would have seen the wisdom in taking action. However, this was not the time nor the place to worry about the past.

If that was not enough, he moved back to his desk and reread the current daily reports of unfathomable atrocities occurring in the city. The reports described soldiers, or parts of soldiers, Russian and German, being found torn to shreds. At first, he shrugged off the reports as fabrications too unbelievable to comprehend, but they kept coming in. He thought it might be some of the citizens, caught in battle, and turning to cannibalism. He dismissed that idea as the reports indicated that the majority of the blood from the corpses was drained, and body parts were spread around in an orderly fashion as if to indicate some type of warning. He also had not heard from Colonel Gough in weeks. Where was he? Why had he not reported in? If he were dead, the Russians would have broadcast the news. Nothing. He sat back down contemplating the future.

* * *

Svetlana examined where the bullet pierced Elizabeth's cheek. The wound was almost completely healed. The damage to the spinal cord would take another day or two to repair.

"What are you doing, Mother?"

"Only checking to see how your wound is healing."

"It is fine. Have your motherly instincts finally awakened?"

Svetlana retreated to Dina's side and stroked her hair. "At least one of my daughters cares about me."

Elizabeth stood to stretch and take in the approaching dawn. The sky to the east contained a red, hazy hue as the sun's rays fought to pierce the smoke-filled horizon.

"I would not be so sure about that. When she is old enough, she too will know who you are." She let out a small laugh, took in a deep breath, then froze. "It is getting closer. I can feel his presence and power. Today is going to be a new dawn for all of us!" She let out an ear-splitting howl.

Svetlana stood up, trying to detect what her daughter was tuned into.

"Who is coming? What does he want?"

"My mate. To rule and conquer."

"Mate? Conquer what? The Germans?"

"Only a small mind would ask such pointless questions, Mother. He and I will do what you, Father, and the Boirarskys only dreamed of. Together, he and I will form a clan that neither human nor vampire will ever defeat!" She let out another howl.

\* \* \*

Otto continued to move through the debris and ruins. Several men attempted to stop him, threatening dire consequences only to become victims of his hunger and rage. He was on a mission, and nothing was going to stand in his way.
*There. There it is again. I am close.*

\* \* \*

Vasily was jarred from his rest with the second howl. He crept forward to the edge of his nest. He detached the scope and panned the city blocks, making sure he stayed in the shadows so the rising sun's light would not reflect off the lens.
"My God! What is that?"

\* \* \*

Colonel Gough had had enough of this accursed place. It was time for him to finish his mission and return to his estate. He knew the shot he fired yesterday found its mark. Today, when he was rested enough, he would venture over to the building to verify the kill. It had to be the quarry he was assigned to kill. Once he confirmed the kill, he would return to von Paulus and demand he be flown out on the next available flight. It did not matter that the city was surrounded; he still believed he was a vital cog in the Third

Reich, and his superior would not let his talents be wasted away in a Russian POW camp or worse.

He amazed himself how he had acclimated to the dirt, filth, and lice that were now his everyday companions. He picked a fat one off his sleeve and crushed it. He could live with that. What he could not deal with were the meager rations he scraped up around the city. It was time to get out so he could sit in front of a plate loaded with potato cakes, sauerbraten, schnitzel, strudel, and a stein of beer. After the meal, he would sit by the large fireplace with his father, smoking a cigar and detailing his great exploits, then retiring for a well-deserved night's sleep in his feather bed.

The piercing howl interrupted his fantasy. At first, he thought the howl was from a man. He heard it again. That was no man. The howl/scream was higher pitched.

*What the hell is going on now?*

\* \* \*

Otto burst into the room. His eyes scanned it, settling on Svetlana. "Where is she?"

She cautiously rose to her feet. "Who are you?"

"Woman, where is she? Tell me now or die!"

Elizabeth appeared in a doorway. "I have been waiting for you."

"You are the woman I seek?"

"Yes."

"Who are the other two?"

"Nothing to concern yourself over." He cast a quick glance at them.

"Then why are you with them?" He noticed the crease mark on her cheek.

"Not by choice."

"Did she do that to you?"

Before she could answer or react, he moved to Svetlana's right side; his left hand firmly gripping her neck and raising her off the floor.

"Then they must be eliminated. They stand in the way of our plans."

Svetlana tried to break his grasp to no avail. Elizabeth approached him, never taking her eyes from his. "She did not do this. It was another who is still out there lurking and hunting in the shadows. Like most humans, he is a coward. Together, I suggest we have our own hunt."

He released his grip dropping Svetlana to the ground. She crumpled like a rotten sack of potatoes, gasping for breath.

"Where is the swine?"

"Patience, my man. Patience. I know how to draw him out."

"Are there any others I should dispose of?"

"There is another out there, but he is a friend of the family. You will not touch him. He will inform his superiors of our actions. Repeat, he is a friend and not to be harmed."

"Is he human?"

"Yes."

"Why should I listen to you?"

"We are equals with a common goal; conquer and rule. But before we proceed, I need to know one thing."

He began to relax a little. "What?"

"Your name."

"Otto. And yours?"

"Elizabeth."

He glanced to his right. "And them?"

"My mother, Svetlana and sister, Dina."

A suppressed memory seeped into his conscious mind. He could see children playing in a park. Mothers pushing strollers. Dogs chasing balls. Laughter filled his head until he reached out to them. They all stopped and stared at him in horror. Within seconds, the cloudless sky filled with dark, ominous thunderheads. Lightning fired down to the ground scorching everything it touched: trees, benches, light poles, and people. They violently exploded with each finger of white-hot lightning. Rather than being frightened of the scene, he embraced it until a voice shrouded his thoughts. *Heim Kommen. Heim Kommen.*

"What purpose do they serve?"

"They can help us in catching our quarry."

"We do not need their help."

"Yes, we do. They will act as bait while we move into position for the capture."

"Capture? Why?"

His question caught her off guard. Instead of providing a quick answer she needed to think over her idea. *Why did I say capture? What purpose could this German provide them in the future? What advantages would they gain with his presence?* For months, she tolerated her mother and sister, knowing all along she would leave them. They only dragged her down. She was designed to be an independent entity, and now was in the presence of one almost like her. Together they would be unstoppable or so she hoped.

She had heard her mother talk of the Minsk Massacre and how her mother avenged the death of her brother, Stephan. It was a grisly tale, even for her, but it taught her that despite all their powers and strengths, they did have a weakness that was deadly.

"I cannot answer that right now. I do know that in order for us to achieve our goals, we will require the help of humans despite how repugnant the thought may be."

"I have no use for anyone other than myself and you!"

Elizabeth walked up to him, slashing him across the face with her talons.

"Woman!"

She thrust her right foot into his crotch, then rammed

both fists into his stomach, launching him across the room and crashing into a concrete wall. Dust and debris rained down on him and spilled out the window.

* * *

Vasily and Gough watched the spectacle through their respective scopes wondering who and what was fighting in the building.

* * *

Otto stood up shaking the debris away. "Woman, that was your first and last mistake. When I am done, you and your family will be nothing but mudholes under my boots!" He let out another howl as his body began transforming. Elizabeth answered in kind. Their howls were threatening to bring the entire structure down on their heads.

Svetlana knew she did not have much time to attempt to defuse the atmosphere. The sounds of Elizabeth and Otto's transformations were frightening. It sounded like a hundred steam engines hurling towards her. She did not know what or how she could stop this slaughter; she only knew she had to try.

Otto's size tripled; he bristled with thick gray muscles. Veins protruded from every appendage. His eyes were black orbs of death. Red saliva poured from his mouth revealing three-inch razor-sharp teeth. It was not only the incisors; all of his teeth took on the same hideous characteristic.

He grabbed a ten-foot wooden beam swinging it over his head. As he charged Elizabeth, with fire in his eyes, he was knocked off his feet.

"Leave my daughter alone!" rang in his ears.

His body crashed into a wall. Splinters of concrete filled the air. He was momentarily stunned. Shaking his head, his eyes lasered in on a form lying five meters from him. It was moving slowly to its feet.

"You will honor my daughter or die by my hands," it hissed.

He stood up, shaking the rubble from his body. "Otto takes what Otto wants. And right now, I choose to take you."

He took a step and was knocked to the floor again. Stars swirled in his eyes as he attempted to refocus.

"If anyone is going to dispose of my mother it will be me, Otto."

"And me," chimed a third voice.

He pulled himself to his feet, surveying the situation. "If I want, I could eliminate all three of you with one mighty stroke. I am the ideal Aryan soldier. I have been ordained to lead the German people to greatness and destroy the Communist scum that infects the land. I will kill anyone who stands in the way of my mission. No mortal can stop me. It is my destiny and I will fulfill it. I will not let three females stand in the way!" His eyes locked on Elizabeth's. Something stirred deep inside. It was an unusual feeling. He felt his knees buckle a touch. His blood began boiling in his veins as it surged through his body. She took a few cautious steps towards him, her eyes never leaving his.

"We are alike, yet different. You have been genetically altered while I am natural. You are a cruel experiment from your masters. I am a product of pure blood. You wish to destroy everything in your path. I choose to eliminate those who deserve it."

She could feel a heightened sense of magnetism the closer she got to him. Her words came faster and less succinct.

"But all of that can wait for another day. Right now, I want one thing and one thing only—YOU!"

She lunged at him sending them crashing through the wall into another room.

"AND I WANT IT ALL RIGHT NOW!"

They wrestled on the floor clawing and tearing at each other. Svetlana and Dina approached the opening in the wall transfixed on the two.

"No, Elizabeth. It's too early!"

Her words were answered with a large piece of the wooden support beam flying towards her.

"I shall do as I wish, Mother!" howled Elizabeth.

"And I shall take what I want!" yelled Otto.

Svetlana and Dina retreated to their hiding nest and waited.

Elizabeth and Otto kept maneuvering for the most advantageous position to attack the other. Blood, hair, and hide flew through the air as they slashed and tore at one another. Otto picked her up and slammed her to the floor. Instead of jumping on his prey and taking her, he held his hands up and howled at the top of his lungs bringing down a shower of dust and concrete.

Arching her back, she vaulted from the floor, sprung onto his chest, and sank her teeth deep into his shoulder blade.

"You are mine! Take me now!" she screamed.

Svetlana and Dina covered their ears as best they could to ward off the cries of ecstasy pouring from the room. Never had she heard such intense mating sounds before. They eclipsed those of Nicole and Dmitri, and even of her and Nikoli. She had hoped to tell her the risks of mating when the time was right. Now, it was too late. She doubted if she would have listened to her.

* * *

Vasily and Gough watched and listened with great interest. Both were perplexed and frightened by the sounds that kept echoing off the surrounding buildings. They also noticed there had been no gunfire over the last few hours as the spectacle played itself out. They could make out steel helmets and soft hats moving around in the previously excellent unobserved hiding places in the piles of rubble lining the streets. They detected forbidden wisps of smoke rising from pipes and lit cigarettes as all those within earshot of the show took a break from the war and pondered what was happening in the building.

A last piercing plural howl had them all taking shelter again.

\* \* \*

Two hours later, they walked back into the room where Svetlana and Dina were resting.

Svetlana could not help but notice they were holding hands. She also saw a crude dressing on Otto's shoulder.

Elizabeth took the lead. "Mother, we are now one. We are the new order. We shall decide who lives and who dies. We will be the masters of the land. We answer only to ourselves. All others are beneath us. Will you join us or resist?"

Svetlana thought it over for a few moments. "Before I answer, Dina and I need to make a mud patch for Otto's wound. Even though he may have amazing healing powers, the wound could become infected and take many months to heal, impeding his abilities. With your permission, I would like to dress the wound properly."

She nodded in agreement but reiterated, "Join us, or die."

# Chapter 17

# Capture

Elizabeth laid out the plan. It was simple. She and Otto would move to the roof of the building at night. Leap over to the adjoining structure where they knew the German was hiding. Otto believed the Russian should also be eliminated. To him, they were the same. It was a heated debate until she convinced him he was not the enemy but a friend of the Romanov's. After she explained how she was wounded, Otto agreed to take revenge on the man who shot her. For the moment, the Russian was safe.

They would capture the German and bring him back to their quarters then decide what to do with him.

* * *

Dina gathered enough dirt and water for Svetlana to tend to Otto's wound. The gash was deeper than the one she had inflicted on Nikoli so many years ago. She could see the muscles and tendons had started to rejuvenate as she applied the salve. Svetlana was amazed at his recuperative powers. As she tended to the wound, a tear crept down her cheek as she remembered not being able to save Stephan.

A small laugh interrupted her concentrations.

"What are you laughing at, Elizabeth?"

"You, Mother. Who would have thought you could show any type of emotion? Did you shed tears when Nikoli evicted you?"

"That is none of your concern, and I am not crying. I have had trouble with this eye for decades."

She applied the last of the paste.

"Done. Now you need to rest. It should properly heal in a few days." She sat back beside Dina, staring into the fading evening twilight. A cold wind blew through the opening cascading a few snow flurries.

"Mother, Oto and I are going out tonight to capture the vile German who shot me."

"Are you sure that is wise?"

"Does it matter? We are going to show this "master race" who is actually in charge."

"What of the Russian?"

"He is safe. I explained to Otto he is only fighting to protect his country and is no threat to us."

Svetlana stared at Otto. "Is this true?"

He rubbed the bandage, pleased with her repair. "It does not matter if it is true or not. It is what we are going to do. My belly and my brain are too full of Aryan superiority dogma. I have no love for those who experimented on me and attempted to kill my bride. He will learn as will many others that they are mice among men. I, not they, am the dominant species. They will soon learn that their pathetic teachings are nothing more than useless rhetoric. Hitler, Himmler, and Goebbels claim to be the ancestors of a lost Aryan breed that used to roam this insignificant planet. That they, through God, have been ordained to rule all the subhuman races and replace them with a pure German bloodline. How can a pathetic corporal, a mild-mannered chicken farmer, and a cripple lead anyone? The only true bloodline is the one she and I carry. We shall introduce a new order the world has never seen."

"I am pleased you have it all figured out."

The sarcastic remark did not escape Elizabeth.

"Mother, I suggest you watch your tongue. It would not be wise to antagonize my husband."

"Husband? You think you two are a couple? I thought the same of Nikoli, and you see how that turned out."

Otto's eyes began flashing fire.

"I am nothing like your insignificant Nikoli!" He took a few steps towards Svetlana.

"Enough!" commanded Elizabeth.

"Mother, in time you and I will have a long talk about what the future holds, but for the moment we need you and Dina to provide a diversion tonight."

"And what would that be?"

"We need you two to man the nest and keep the attention of the German while we execute the capture. Think you can handle that simple task?"

"We will do our best."

"No. You will excel at the task assigned, or the warning I spoke of earlier will occur sooner than you might like. Understood?"

She nodded her head in agreement.

"I did not hear you."

"We will execute your orders flawlessly."

"That is better. Now, we are going to rest for a few hours. I suggest you do the same."

\* \* \*

Rudolph was ready to leave the rat-infested city. For three months he crawled through the ruins searching for his target. He never thought the day would come when he wearied of s hunt, but it had. Day after day he searched for the lone sniper who was demoralizing his fellow soldiers. It was the first time he acknowledged to himself that the war was bigger than him and his rifle. It was a joint mission and it would take all of them to beat the Russians and return to their beloved *fatherland* and victory.

The city was surrounded and he could feel the claws of the Russian Army squeezing the life out of the 6$^{th}$ Army. He knew it was only a matter of time before he would be recalled to Berlin to serve a more important function. He was too valuable to have his life wasted in the piles of rubble. It was fine for the common soldier, but not for him. Yet, he could not leave without killing his opponent.

In all the hunts he participated in, this would be his finest accomplishment. When he finished this assignment, he would be a hero of the Third Reich, and more than likely invited to join Himmler's inner circle. The thought of hobnobbing with the elite was not the ultimate goal. He had met Hitler, Goebbels, Keitel, Goering, and others. They were a pathetic group of imbeciles fumbling about in their own glory. No, they would be the privileged ones with him as the guest of honor. He would mesmerize them with his tales of the hunt and how his superior skills proved too much for his subhuman opponent. They would all marvel at the Knight's Cross with the oak-leaf cluster and diamonds, decorating his neck, wishing they could have earned one themselves. Yes, he would be the toast of Berlin, and they would pay a handsome fee to be in his company.

First things first—it was time to end the hunt.

\* \* \*

Vasily positioned himself so the faint moonlight crept into his hideout, illuminating his watch and logbook. He took the mental notes he made over the last hours and started putting them down. He was careful not to embellish too much, but it would be difficult. How does one describe the sights and sounds over the last hours of waning sunlight? Who would believe his tale? He must try. Others must know. If not them, then for his own personal recollections when the years marched forward, and his memory faded.

*Activity in the building to the NE, approx. two hundred meters. Shot fired at 16:00 hours towards building. No visible hits. Cries from building at 18:00. Horrific sounds echoed in the square. Dust and debris fell out of building.*

*20:00 Loud ear-piercing howling filled my eardrums. Not of an earthly being. Skin tingled with needles. More loud screeching and crying. More debris flying out of openings. Quiet now reigns over the city. It is an unsettling quiet. No sounds of battle. Even the rats have sought cover. I have never faced or known fear until this night. Something or someone is stalking the hunters. I need rest but fear it could be my last.*

He reread the entry, shaking his head in disbelief. *What sane person would believe these ramblings?* He closed the book, tucked it back in his pocket, and tried to get comfortable as the cold of Stalingrad seeped into his bones. He panned the building across the street looking for his prey. His gaze rested on two pairs of eyes boring into him. They were brilliant, fiery orbs of red and green. He couldn't take his eyes off them. He felt he was in a dream being drawn to the objects. They appeared to be getting larger and larger the longer he watched. The trance broke when his peripheral vision detected two shadows flashing through the air.

\* \* \*

Rudolph scanned the buildings looking for his opponent. He knew he was there. He could feel his presence; he knew he was close. But he was too smart to show himself for long. In fact, he had no idea where his adversary was.

The city was slowly weighing on him. His skill and concentration were being sucked out of him; they were eroding day by day. It was time to end the madness; time to return home to his hearth and cognac. It was time to get the hell out of Stalingrad!

He peered intensely through the ruins, desperate to discover his foe's hiding place so he could put one bullet neatly between his eyes and leave. Instead of finding one pair, he came across two pairs boring in on him. He blinked and wiped his eyes, convinced he was hallucinating. He looked again. The pair seemed closer. They were a dark, throbbing purple and green. They drew him in. Instead of reaching for his rifle, he could only stare as the orbs came closer and closer. Rudolph moved an inch forward for a better look. He could not take his eyes off those staring at him. The more he focused, the larger they appeared. He blinked once more, and they were gone. He panned his eyes back and forth trying to find them. Concrete dust filtered down on him. As he attempted to wipe the dust away, the air rushed out of his lungs. His vision went black.

"You bastard. You will pay for your transgressions!"

\* \* \*

Vasily tried to follow the shadows, but they were too fast. Still, he was not letting his guard down. That is one thing the city had taught him. How many men had he shot who believed they were in a safe area? How many officers fell to his finger when they were only trying to relieve themselves? He had lost count.

The hairs on his neck rose. An unknown foul odor filled his nostrils. He felt like vomiting but suppressed it.

"Do not move," came a hoarse, gravely voice. "My mother says you are a friend of the family. Because of that, it was agreed your life is to be spared. However, if you try to follow us, we will think nothing of killing you. Understood?"

He nodded.

"Good. The German you have been hunting is now in our hands. He is no longer your concern. Understood?"

It was difficult to make out each word, but he knew enough not to disagree. Again, he nodded.

"Good."

It took a few minutes for the air to clear and his heart rate to return to normal. He took a deep breath of the clean, crisp air then collapsed into a well-deserved sleep. He was still alive, but for how long?

# Chapter 18

# The Brewery

"It is time. Are all our preparations in place?" queried Nikoli.

"Yes. The flowerpot was in the window last night, and our guard is still working the same shift. Jacub does not seem as nervous as he was a week ago. He appears to be in much better physical condition." replied Corporal Schmidt.

"How can you tell?"

"He is no longer slinking around and hunched over. He is walking with an authority I never thought him capable of. He actually told off a guard when he did not produce the proper papers when entering the complex."

"Really? What an interesting turn of events. Perhaps I underestimated our old friend."

"Perhaps."

A thin smile came over his lips. *Is it possible Jacub was becoming one of them? If so, how would they be greeted?* He would find out when they met again.

"Good. It is time to don our uniforms and become one of the master race."

As he changed into his captured general's uniform, he marveled at how easily they acquired it. The general and his aide were drinking at a local tavern spending their hard-earned money on some of the town's women. Like most of their colleagues, they failed to entice the local Fräuleins with their advances but were promised next time. At around midnight, they departed with visions of large breasts and soft warm legs wrapping around them the next time they returned. Leaving in a state of euphoria and alcoholic bliss, they sped down the narrow, deserted streets shouting obscenities at the empty buildings.

When the headlights revealed a figure standing in the middle of the road, the general urged his driver to smash the insignificant rodent from their path. The driver pushed the pedal to the floor accelerating towards the person. As the figure became clearer in his blurry eyesight, fear gripped him. What was becoming clearer was neither human or beast. It was a cross. He slammed on the brakes throwing the general against the seat, knocking him unconscious. As the car skidded to an abrupt stop, he was never given a chance to challenge the intruder, for as he rolled down the window, the creature was upon him, yanking him out and crushing his windpipe. As much as it pained him, he honored Nikoli's instruction that the uniform must not be damaged or soaked in blood.

With the driver disposed of, Corporal Schmidt opened the back door, grabbed the general, and snapped his neck. He motioned to Nikoli that the task was completed. They undressed the men, sucked them dry, relieved them of their papers, stuffed them into the trunk, and returned home. It was a successful mission. His first!

Now it was time for a more complex assignment.

* * *

"-Nikoli, all is in order."

"Schmidt, is everything in place? Have we overlooked anything?"

Corporal Schmidt examined their uniforms making sure there was no blood or tears on them. All the ribbons were in the correct place, and most importantly, the new IDs would not be questioned. It took some time to convince the local document officer to provide new photos for him and Nikoli. After depositing $200.00 in Reichsmarks and a flash of his incisors, the man asked no more questions. In less than four hours, the new papers were ready and beyond reproach. The bureaucrat proudly produced the new papers to General Kurt Heineman and Sergeant Gunther Brandenburg. Pleased with the man's work, he gave him another $200 Reichsmarks.

"And the car, Corporal Schmidt?"

"It too is in excellent condition and working order."

"Good. We leave in the morning."

\*\*\*

The car edged up to the gate. He chuckled when he read the sign over the entrance. "Arbeit Macht Frei." The guard approached them. "Papers."

They both produced them.

The guard took a cursory look. "They are in order, Herr General. Park the car by the administration building. You will be met there and taken to the commandant." He saluted then turned to the other guards. "Raise the gate. Let them pass."

Today's purpose was not to free the inmates but to perform more reconnaissance in order to plan the upcoming mission.

Schmidt brought the car to a stop, exited, and opened the door for Nikoli. Jacub was standing outside the building with the commandant. He noticed they were talking in subdued tones.

The commandant came down the steps briskly.

"Welcome to my camp, Herr General. My name is Colonel Hapsburg. I will be your guide today. I only wish you would have called earlier. I could have had a more palatable menu available, and the orchestra would have welcomed you with a performance worthy of your rank."

"Perhaps next time. My function today is to examine how the camp is working and if it is running at peak efficiency."

"Understood, Herr General. Please, come to my office. I will brief you on how the inmates are sorted and selected for work details."

"Excellent. I look forward to your report."

The smell of burnt flesh wafted by his nose. *This too shall pass.*

\* \* \*

They entered the colonel's small but comfortable office. A portrait of Hitler was on the wall behind the desk, flanked by the SS and swastika flag. The acrid smell of cheap German cigarette smoke covered the room. The chairs seemed out of place; they were large and comfortable. He could tell they were filled with horsehair as he settled down.

"The spoils of war, Herr General. I hope to have the desk and anteroom filled with much more suitable furniture in the coming months. You know how slow supply requests are being filled even though there is an overabundance filling our warehouses." He chuckled with his comment. Nikoli fumed. "But what is one to do? There is a war going on and we all have to make concessions, don't we?"

"I do not," barked back Nikoli. "Now, shall we get down to business? I am a busy man and have no time for idle chatter."

"Yes, Herr General. My apologies. Would you like a cup of ersatz or some pastries before we begin?"

"No. Get on with it."

"Of course, Herr General. Please accept my apologies."

Nikoli rose from the chair. "Apologize to me one more time, Colonel, and I will either have you transferred to where the real fighting is going on or make you one of the inmates of this facility. Understood?"

A bead of sweat rolled down the colonel's face. "Jawohl."

"Good." He sat back down. "Proceed."

\* \* \*

Nikoli never put much stock in time passing by. In mortal years, he was over three hundred years old, and in all that time he never once worried about the hours in a day or how many minutes composed an hour. He often scoffed at those who did wear watches. Time was not a commodity one could control thus worrying about seconds and minutes ticking off was a futile undertaking, until now.

The colonel rattled on for over three hours on the operations of the camp. The way he knew was the incessant clicking of the grandfather clock in the room. Each tick was hammering his brain. The sound reminded him of a poorly performed Wagner opera where the conductor did not have a clue as to time or rhythm.

The only nuggets of information he cataloged were how many inmates the compound could hold and the amount of cargo being delivered each week.

He was sickened with the colonel's cavalier descriptions of the children being ripped from their mothers' arms and sent to the showers. Was it that long ago when he witnessed those actions himself and believed he could work in harmony with the new occupiers? How foolish he felt reminding himself of the tentative agreement. For the first time in his life, he was face-to-face with the emotions of guilt, remorse, and embarrassment. He dismissed the thought from his mind; he must focus on the job at hand.

The size of the camp had tripled since he last entered it. Security was at a premium. Over two hundred guards patrolled the fence line inside and out, making sure no passersby stumbled onto this camp of death or attempted to flee its confines.

He took note that it could handle over one hundred thousand inmates a month. More if necessary. Each week at least five thousand new recipients were processed. That meant that at least twenty thousand a month were being exterminated or outright murdered. Many died from starvation, typhus, tuberculosis, or exhaustion. Others were disposed of by torture for the amusement of the guards. Some of the unlucky ones, if there were such a thing, were assigned to the medical department for experimental treatments and sterilization.

He was impressed with the efficiency of how the camp operated. When a train pulled in, the selection process began. Children were sent directly to the showers as they were too young or weak to provide a true function for their masters.

The men and women were split up into two groups: the healthy and the old. If an inmate appeared the slightest bit ill, they were also sent to the showers. Those remaining were stripped naked, then inspected by an array of guards and officers. The women who showed promise of performing for the guards were put in a select group for future assignment.

The groups were shuttled into lines where they queued up to be shaven, deloused, tattooed, then clothed with a garment that was thinner than a pair of pajamas. They were assigned a barracks and given a wooden bowl. They were effectively stripped of all their humanity, decency, and self-respect.

Nikoli was furious with this waste of food and utter disregard for life itself. At one time, he questioned his motive for what he was proposing to undertake; now he knew why he must follow through. When he accomplished the mission, he would make sure the colonel, and those like him, were saved for a special exercise. One they would not soon forget, if they survived.

"Herr General. Did you hear me?" "Herr General?'

Nikoli cleared his senses. "What?"

"I was asking if you were hungry? We usually eat around this time."

He glanced at the clock. 1:00pm. "No. But I would like to tour the compound."

"Herr General. My staff and I would be only too pleased to show you the camp, but I believe it would be best performed on a full stomach and a glass of wine."

Nikoli rose from his chair. "Colonel, either you will give me a tour, or my guard and I will provide one for ourselves. And, I wish for the camp administrator to join us."

"Jacub Polasky? But why? What information could he provide that I cannot?"

"Colonel, what better person to join us than the one responsible for the mass amount of cargo you handle on a daily basis. Other than your daily reports you read, who else knows the ins and outs of the camp better than the person who is responsible for the daily operations?"

"I still do not think he will be of much service, Herr General."

Nikoli's eyes bore into the colonels. For a moment, he thought he detected an unusual flash in the general's eyes. "As you wish."

\* \* \*

What Nikoli witnessed was in stark contrast to the immaculate clean surroundings where he entered. The gate was of excellent ornamental ironwork. The guard shack and buildings were neat and orderly with a fresh coat of paint. He noticed the barracks three hundred meters to the south but thought nothing of them. They were in neat rows reminding him of typical army barracks. Fresh flowers and gardens were abundant; they flanked the entrance to the colonel's office. Even the few inmates he had seen tending to the grounds appeared to be in good trim and spirits for being prisoners. The vacant look in their eyes bothered him not. He had seen the look many times over the ages when the armies he fought with were victorious and took the conquered to tend to their needs. But there was something unnatural about the way they walked.

They did not move about as people who had capitulated; they were more lethargic and methodical. They did not walk, but shuffled in a strange monotonous rhythm. Hand movements were slow and agonizing as if they were trying to conserve energy.

"Colonel, before we proceed, I have a question."

"Of course, Herr General."

"Why do the prisoners move as they do?"

"I am not sure I understand the question, Herr General."

"They move with purpose but appear to be purposeless. Their actions are slow and painful. Why?"

"Herr General, is that all?" He let out a laugh. "They know they are a beaten people and understand who their true masters are. For decades, they infected all of Europe with their wealth, religion, and politics. Everything they touched was ruined. Look at how they were responsible for that vile Versailles Treaty. If not for them, we would have defeated the French and British and would have begun the cleansing twenty years ago. Instead, they forced us to live in poverty and filth. They forced their will on us, and now it is our turn to correct their mistakes of the past. Yes, Herr General, they are learning to follow and obey their true masters."

Nikoli shook his head.

"Jacub. Do you feel the same way?"

"Nikoli, truth be known…" Before he could finish, a right hand connected with his jaw.

"You will address me as Herr General, you swine."

Jacub rubbed the growing welt, knowing he had almost exposed his colleague.

"My apologies, Herr General. I forgot my place."

"Indeed. Do not let it happen again."

"Excuse me, Herr General. How did he know your first name? Most peculiar." His eyes began darting between the two.

Jacub rubbed his sore jaw. "It was my mistake, Herr Colonel. The last inmate I processed was named Nikoli. I should not work so many hours as it appears fatigue is taking its toll."

The colonel came within half a meter of Jacub. "One more mistake like that and fatigue will be the least of your worries. Understood?"

"Yes, Herr Colonel."

"Good. Now, answer the general's question."

He glanced at Nikoli who nodded. "I agree with the colonel's assessment. We are a defeated people and are learning to submit to our new masters."

"I see." He looked about the grounds, detecting a whiff of smoke to the northwest of the parade grounds. "Let us proceed."

They walked another fifty meters before coming to a second gate. It was twelve feet tall and made of cheap wood. Barbed wire was strung on the top and at two-foot horizontal lines from top to bottom. Guard towers were stationed every fifty meters with at least two guards posted. They were manning 7.92mm machine guns along with sidearms. He noticed a barren area approximately five meters wide. Where it ended another fence began.

The fresh air at the colonel's office was being overridden by a stench of decaying, burnt flesh. The odor was irritating to his heightened senses.

"Schmidt. Does this look familiar?"

"Nein."

"Keep your eyes open."

"Jawohl."

The colonel stepped forward. "Guard, open the gate."

"Papers, Herr Colonel."

He produced them.

"And who are you bringing with you, Herr Colonel?'

"These are guests from Berlin. They are here to assess how efficient our operation is."

"This is highly unusual, Herr Colonel. I will need to see their papers also."

'Understood. Good to see you are taking your posting seriously. Exterminating vermin can be a monotonous assignment." Each of the men smiled.

Did Nikoli hear him correctly? *Extermination?*

"Gentlemen, your papers please."

Each one handed them over. The guard thoroughly checked them for authenticity. When it came to Schmidt's, they were in order, but something seemed off. What, he could not place for the moment. The ID said, Sergeant Gunther Brandenburg from Alsace-Lorraine. Even though the picture matched, there was an unusual familiarity nagging in the back of his mind. He kept looking at the picture and Schmidt.

"Is there a problem, Corporal?" asked Nikoli.

"No, sir. I thought I recognized the sergeant. My mistake. Herr Colonel, all the papers are in order. You may pass."

"Danke, Corporal. I will mention you in my report. Your fine work will garner a promotion and perhaps a new post with our victorious armies in the east."

"Danke, Herr Colonel."

The men passed through the gate and into hell.

*  *  *

The stench became overwhelming. Never had Nikoli felt the need to vomit until now. What he at first thought were ghosts, were humans. He could not tell whether they were male or female; they were walking skeletons at best. The shuffles from the inmates tending the gardens were nonexistent. These figures barely moved. Average weight could not have been more than forty kilos. Heads were shaven bare. Eyes were sunk deep in the sockets. There was no color in the pupils. He noticed many of them were urinating or defecating as they walked. One unfortunate prisoner performed the act as he passed two guards. One knocked him to the ground then struck him in the face with the butt of his rifle. His companion removed his pistol and shot him in the head. No one raised a hand or went to provide assistance. Rather, they walked around him as if nothing had happened. Within minutes, inmates with a wheelbarrow showed up and loaded the body. It took both men to handle what was nothing more than a skeletal frame covered in skin. The colonel never gave the incident a second look.

"This is their punishment for trying to enslave us to their will. Gentlemen, would you like to visit one of the barracks?"

"Yes," replied Nikoli.

It was the vilest building he had ever entered. The putrid stench of filth, feces, and death enveloped his senses. His gut retched multiple times, but there was no bile to force out.

He could count eight bodies stacked like cordwood in a space designed for two. At first, he thought they were all dead till he saw them attempt to move. Even though there was little light in the room, his eyes saw more than he wanted. The apathy and hopelessness filled them. He could detect lice moving about the bodies, feeding at will for their hosts had neither the energy or care to ward them off.

"You filthy, worthless Jews. We, the German people, have provided you with acceptable living accommodations and this is how you take care of it? You will pay for your transgressions by cleaning up this filth with your tongues! Do you hear me?"

One man sat up. "No. Do it yourself."

"Who said that?" railed the colonel. "If you do not come forward, I will send the entire barrack to the showers! Do you hear me? Answer me, you swine!"

The exchange fascinated Nikoli. These people had no humanity left. They had no hope, but they still had a sense of will and being.

"I will only ask one more time." He removed his Luger. "Who dares to defy my authority? Which dog chose to bark at the wrong master?"

A thin, wiry figure pulled himself from the bunk. "I did, Herr Colonel. I, Hiram Rabinowitz of Krakow said it. I, a man of deep faith and belief challenged you."

The colonel leveled his pistol. Before he could pull the trigger, a hand gripped his arm. Rather, a steel claw clamped down forcing him to wince. "Wait." He lowered his gun.

Nikoli stepped towards the man.

"Do you know who you are talking to?"

"Yes."

"Who?"

"Men who call themselves the master race. Men who have no allegiance to God, but only to themselves. Men, who when this war is over, will pay for their crimes against humanity. That is who I am talking to."

"You realize you could be shot for what you are saying?"

"Yes. But death comes to all of us in one form or another. My people and I turned our backs to God and are being reminded why we must be faithful in him and not ourselves. Our people have suffered persecution since the day Christ was crucified. We were given a choice by Pontius Pilate, Jesus or Barabbas. We chose Barabbas. My people will always be persecuted wherever we go."

"That is enough, you pig!" yelled the colonel.

Nikoli raised his hand. "Colonel, this is a man of education worth saving. Jacub, do you require an assistant? Did you not mention earlier of your heavy workload?"

"Yes, I did."

"Excellent. Then it is settled. Colonel, Mr. Rabinowitz is Jacub's new assistant effective immediately. Understood?"

"Jawohl, Herr General. As you wish."

"Good. Let us continue with the tour."

The most appalling yet fascinating building was the crematorium. The efficiency was typical of German organization. Even though the guards were not performing the acts of burning the bodies, they kept a close eye on those who were. If they stumbled or slipped up, they were pushed into the furnaces and burned alive.

"How many do you process a day, Colonel?"

"Seventy-five an hour, but that is not enough. I have four more ovens on order that can double our capacity and keep up with the demand. I should be receiving them in two to four weeks. It depends on train schedules and the availability of rolling stock. Right now, for some reason, all rolling stock has been diverted to the armed forces. Do they not know what important work we are doing behind the lines? I have sent a personal request to Herr Himmler to remedy this inconvenience."

"Colonel, I shall pass on your request when I next see him. Will that be sufficient?"

"Herr General, I would be humbled if you would do that. Danke."

Nikoli scanned the compound, amazed at the size. When he first planned this, he could not fathom what would be involved. He knew it would take more than him, Schmidt, and Jacub.

He glanced at his watch. "Colonel, the hour is getting late and I must be getting back to my command. I have seen enough and will file a complete, favorable report to the Reichsführer."

The colonel led them back to the security gate with a quickened pace.

"Guard, open the gate."

"Jawohl, Herr Colonel. Please present your papers."

"Why?"

"It is regulations, sir."

"I know it's regulations, you dummkopf. Do we resemble the prisoners? Do we look like filthy, Jewish pigs or murderers?"

"Nein, Herr Colonel." He let out a laugh.

"Good lad. Gentlemen, if you please."

The guard gave a cursory look at the IDs until he came across Schmidt's.

"Herr Sergeant. Are you sure we have never met before? Your face is vaguely familiar. I am just having a hard time placing it."

"Corporal. We have never met. If we had, I would have silenced your wagging tongue." The corporal stiffened without backing down.

"I am sure we have met, Sergeant. But for the moment, I cannot remember where or when."

"Perhaps it is better you clear your memory banks before I do it for you." A touch of fire flashed in his right eye.

Nikoli stepped in to defuse the situation.

"Gentlemen. We are all soldiers of the Third Reich. We have a common enemy and it is not each other. When the war is over, if we cross paths again, any past disagreements will be settled then. Agreed?"

Both men meekly nodded.

"Good. Please return our IDs so we may be on our way."

The corporal handed them over.

\*\*\*

The colonel and his staff stood at attention and saluted as Schmidt drove the car through the gate. The immense size of the compound troubled Nikoli. He could complete the plan, but not with the original timetable developed. A simple raid was out. He would need to figure out the following:

1) Neutralizing the guards
2) Train schedules
3) Frontal assault or envelopment
4) Feeding of the inmates
5) Transporting the inmates
6) Clothing the inmates
7) Clearing the camp
8) Destroying the facilities
9) Time of attack
10) Length of attack
11) Securing communications

And the list went on.
"Corporal Schmidt, we are going to need help."
Schmidt looked in the rearview mirror. "Who will help you?"
"That, Corporal Schmidt, is the question, isn't it?"

\*\*\*

Four hours had passed since General Heinemann left. The colonel had enjoyed a hearty dinner and was now enjoying a rich cognac when there was a knock at the door.
"Enter."
The guard from gate two entered.
"Yes. What is it, Corporal?"
"Herr Colonel. I need to report a deserter."

"Who?"

"Sergeant Brandenburg is Corporal Schmidt, sir."

"Are you sure about that charge, Corporal?"

"Yes, Herr Colonel."

"And how do you know him?"

"We served together in the Poland and Denmark campaign. He was my squad leader."

"I see. If he is not who he said he is, then either General Heinemann does not know, or he is not who he claimed to be. What do you think, Sergeant?"

The guard stood stunned with the sudden promotion. "That's correct, Corporal. You were just promoted. Give your full name to my adjutant so the proper paperwork is forwarded to Berlin." He stood up and watched the yard guards herd another load of refugees to their assigned tasks and fates. "As of today, you are now on my personal detail. Your days of dealing with dogs and filthy Jews are finished. Did he show any signs of recognizing you?"

"Nein, Herr Colonel."

"Interesting. Did he get a good look at you?"

"Jawohl, Herr Colonel."

"I am waiting for you to answer my first question."

"I have nothing to add other than I would call your superiors to verify his claim."

"An excellent idea! Yes, I shall verify his identity. But if they are not who they say they are, why would they want a tour of the camp? Very interesting."

"Herr Colonel. There could only be a few options available: sabotage or a mass escape."

"That, Sergeant, is an excellent analysis! Leave me now and do as I instructed. I have much to contemplate."

"Jawohl, Herr Colonel." He clicked his heels, saluted, then left.

Hapsburg lit up another fine cigar digesting the facts he was presented with. He smiled thinking of the next time he and the general would meet again and the reception he would receive.

# Chapter 19

# Returning Home

Traveling through the backcountry was more trying than Dmitri and Nicole imagined. Finding food was not a problem. There was plenty of fresh game and the occasional lost soldier or deserter to feast upon, but it was never enough for the boys. Their appetite was insatiable. If they were not clinging to her breasts every second of every day, they were latching onto her neck for additional sustenance. Dmitri tried several times to have them feed from him, but they would release horrible screeches every time he tried to separate them from her.

They had been hiking for over a month, avoiding as much contact with humans as possible. One look at the couple and people would know they were not of this world or any other they might conjure up.

Dmitri did his best to maintain an even steady pace. Each day he could see the pain in her face and the unevenness of her steps as the boys drained her dry. If she could hold on a few more days, they would be home and able to rest. They just needed to keep going.

Nicole collapsed to the forest floor from exhaustion with their boys gripping on tight.

"Dmitri. I cannot go on any longer. These bastard children are draining me dry."

"You cannot give up now. We are less than two days travel from Bezpieczeństwo. Once there we will be able to rest."

"It will not matter if we make it or not, you fool. No matter what we do they refuse to obey us. I believe it best you leave me behind to die. I will also make sure they die with me."

"The children? You cannot be serious? I will not let you or the boys die! I will see to it!"

She gasped for breath as if it were her last. "How?"

"I do not know, but I will figure it out."

"How indeed is the boy vampire going to save his precious bride and perfect hellions?"

Both of them looked about. Dmitri stood to his feet. "Who said that? Where are you? Show yourself now."

"Now?" came a searing sound. "Now is when I say it is time, not when some pathetic boy attempts to issue commands."

His blood began boiling. He could feel his bones and muscles starting to contort.

"Is the meager boy trying to change? And if you do, what will you do? You cannot see me; only hear me."

"Enough of these games!" roared Dmitri. "Either show yourself or begone with your vile tongue." Coarse hair sprouted from his face. Fire danced in his eyes.

"I see it is time for your first lesson. I hoped you would have chosen to display a more prudent demeanor in your decision to challenge me, but alas, you are a clumsy, foolish group of beings. I should have learned that from Svetlana."

The sound of her mother's name pricked up her senses. "I do not know who you are, but you say you know my mother?"

A harsh laugh pierced the forest. "Good to see one of you has a brain. Now, tell your boy to calm down and revert to his normal form, or I will provide a lesson in manners he will never forget. And if I am not careful, I could knock out one of his feeding teeth. Would that not be a shame, dearie?"

"Dmitri, calm down. We need to hear what this apparition has to say."

His claws began drawing back into his hands. The flames diminished from his eyes.

"That is better."

"Please, show yourself."

"In time, my dear. In time. First, do I understand that the boys are giving you problems you do not know how to treat?"

"Yes."

"And why do you think that is?"

"I have no idea."

"Of course not, because your mother failed to provide all the facts of birthing those horrid creatures. And Kirilli would have done well explaining the situation with his boy child."

The two looked at each other in shock. Whatever it was knew the clans. But how?

"I will explain your questions in time. For the moment, I have an errand to run. Until then, please do me a favor."

"What?" they answered.

"Do not die."

\* \* \*

How much time elapsed, neither one knew. They realized if something was not done in the next few hours, Nicole and the boys would die.

"Do you know if she or it will come back?"

"I wish I knew. How are you feeling?"

"How do I look?"

It was the first time he chose not to gaze upon his wife. He tried to remember her the day they mated—young, beautiful, full of life. What he saw now appeared to resemble a haggard old woman on death's door. Her soft blonde hair was matted; its sheen long since gone. Her once soft, silky skin felt more like dried-out leather. The eyes that once held promise and love were filled with despair and loss. They no longer flickered with light; they were dark circles of hopelessness.

Why had his father not told him everything he needed to know to be a good father and husband? Some day he would get those answers.

"You look tired. Rest for now."

"If I rest any more, I will never wake."

The boys were still clinging to her, sucking the life out of her every cell. He could see her blood surging through their veins as they continued to drain her. He tried to pull one of them off. His attempt was met with an angry cry and a slash across his cheek.

He grabbed it harder, infuriated with the assault.

"I will kill both of you with my bare hands!"

They released their death grip and went after him. One went for his throat, the other his face. Nicole wanted to help him but had not the strength. She could only utter quiet words of disgust and compassion as they began ripping him apart

He pulled the one off that was tearing his throat open and flung it to the ground. The other yelled in anger at his brother's fate and continued to gnaw on Dmitri's face more furiously.

Black blood oozed from the open wounds covering his face and chest. His energy level diminished with each bite and scrape. Nicole could only look on in horror and sadness. Being a mom was what she had always dreamed of. She thought it would be wonderful raising children in her vision; she never expected this. She glanced at the child lying by the tree. It began stirring. Its eyes were wild and darting around. She looked up when Dmitri let out a cry of pain.

He was able to remove the clawing, thrashing child from his face. What Nicole saw was only a mash of tissue and muscle; his facial features were gone.

"These monsters must die!" He prepared to have it join its brother. He reared back and threw it with all his might at its brother. It stopped in midair and floated to the ground in a state of haze. The other brother was in a crouching position preparing to launch at his father. He lifted off the ground and was laid by his brother.

"You two have much to learn about parenting."

A figure moved to the boys, picked them up, and cradled them. They cooed and smiled as the entity held them.

"It's alright now. Your auntie is here to make things all better, but you must learn to like your mother and father."

Dmitri went to Nicole's side and slid down, exhausted. She began nursing his wounds with a loving touch. They were thankful for the interruption from the stranger.

"Now that I have done what you two are incapable of performing, it is time to teach you what your parents were not able to do." The stranger turned and looked at them.

They thought they were looking at a ghost. The stranger resembled Svetlana in every way, except for her speech.

"Shocked, my dears? Of course, you are, for you have not learned how to see past appearances. You take everything you see at face value; when you can look beyond the obvious, you will recognize what you need to visualize."

"How do you know what my mother looks like?"

The stranger approached, still holding the relaxed brothers. "It is time to tell you the secrets of the past so you will understand the path you are on."

"What path?" sputtered Dmitri as he spit blood out of his mouth.

"Silence! If you wish for your wife to gaze upon you with loving eyes again, you will keep your tongue silent."

She laid the children in Nicole's lap. She shuddered as the boys began crawling about her.

"Do not fret, my dear. They are only trying to get comfortable." She still cringed waiting for them to thrust their fangs into her skin.

"I have no name or origin. I only exist. I knew your fathers and grandfathers many centuries ago. They were an unruly bunch. Instead of remaining in the shadows, they were foolish and thought they could fit in and work with humans. Many times, I laughed at their feeble attempts to rule mankind. They believed their superior strength and healing powers would overcome numbers. They were wrong to the point it almost cost them their lives. They came to me unwillingly and by accident. I promised to help them if they would eliminate the many enemies I have amassed over the years. If they did not, I would throw them back into the sunlight and let their bodies burn to the bone. Or, I would wait till darkness fell and let the townsfolk have their way. Knowing the odds were against them, they wisely agreed to my terms. I gave them a potion which allows your kind to travel in the daylight. Was this never discussed with either of you?"

They shook their heads no.

"No surprise." She gazed at the happy boys. "Let us discuss current events you are not familiar with. Nicole, your father, in his infinite wisdom has managed to become an outcast. Konstantin, Kirilli, and Svetlana want nothing to do with him. Of course, you already knew about your mother's transgressions. Foolish woman." She smirked with the thought. "He is teaming up with a rather unusual ally. One of the first Germans he turned, for some reason, has failed to die which is most perplexing. I shall have to examine this oddity more thoroughly when time allows. Regardless, he is starting to learn patience and empathy, two traits no one, including myself ever thought possible. He is the coldest soul I have ever known. As I mentioned, that is changing. He is appalled with the Germans' liquidation of those they deem undesirable or a drag on their empire. He is planning on freeing as many of the prisoners as possible, but he is discovering what a daunting undertaking it will be, and he cannot do it alone. He will need help and a lot of it. That is where you two come in. You will seek him out when you have returned home and have healed from your wounds." She removed two small vials from her pockets. "Give each child a full bottle. This will alter their blood and allow you to start regaining strength. They will still need to feed on you but not as voraciously." She then produced a worn cloth. "Place this on his face. It will ease the pain and heal the wounds."

Nicole reached up and grabbed the items. "Thank you." She placed the rag on Dmitri's face. "You have not said anything about my mother."

"Ah yes, Svetlana the Seducer."

"Seducer?"

"Yes, dearie. Before she fell to the charms of Nikoli, she was known across Russia for her sexual prowess and appetites. For those who could keep up, they were rewarded with more invitations. Those who could not were thrust out at the end of a whip. Nikoli was the only customer she would beg to return and satisfy her."

"That would explain a lot." She digested the information for a few moments. "Where is she now and what is she doing?"

"She is in a city named Stalingrad with Dina and Elizabeth."

"Elizabeth?"

"Your bastard sister spawned from the seed of the German Eckhardt. The reason Nikoli banished her if you remember."

"He never told us why he threw her out, not that I cared."

"You will start caring now or you will die. This, I promise."

"Why?"

"Elizabeth is a genetic mutation unlike any I have seen. Her strength and intellect far exceed anyone else in the clans. Her emotional makeup is unpredictable, and I fear she is coming into contact with one like her but not like her. It is a creature created out of vampiric blood with genetic mutations I am not familiar with. This, I must remedy. If your mother and true sister survive, we have a chance at survival."

"I am not following you."

"Dearie, the Germans will lose the war; it is only a matter of time. No country can conquer Russia. She is a beast unto herself, and history has shown how unkind she can be with uninvited guests. Too bad Napoleon did not think it through. But then, he did provide us with an ample food supply for a decade." She laughed.

"How do you know all of the things that have, are, and will happen?"

"I can only tell you that my kind were linked with your kind over a millennium ago. How, no one knows, and if they do, it is not talked about. We are the superior beings of this planet but are too weak to lead and conquer. We prefer to stay hidden and appear only when forces of pure evil threaten the balance. Otherwise, we stay to ourselves in the Urals and live as most other Russian peasants do, unseen." The sound of wolves baying in the forest filled the air.

"Child, feed your children with the tonic. Tend to your husband. Return to Bezpieczeństwo and heal."

"Will we see you again?"

"Only if I deem it necessary. Now, do as I say, for time is a commodity in short supply."

She then vanished.

The boys sucked down the bottles, licking the insides dry and falling asleep.

"Dmitri, what do you think of all this?"

"We should do as she says. If a battle is coming, we must prepare. For now, let us sleep and heal. Tomorrow we head home."

# Chapter 20

# Decision

Gough awoke in a haze; he could see nothing. The thought of going blind frightened him to no end. Without his sight, his function in life and to the Third Reich was at an end. He would never feel the sensation of putting a well-placed bullet between the eyes of a target. He would never hunt with his father again, competing with him to replace the fourteen-point buck over the mantle. His eyes would never again gaze on the buxom waitresses he so often flirted with. His life as he knew it was over. There was only one thing to do, and that was to take his own life before the city beat him to it.

He tried to move his hands with no reaction. Then his legs and feet. They too did not respond. If he was restrained, he should feel pressure when he moved—nothing. Was he dead? Is this what death is? An empty nothingness? If he was dead, how did it happen? Who was worthy of extinguishing an esteemed and revered officer of the Third Reich?

His memory flashed back to a childhood moment when his mother and father fought over him attending Catholic school. His mother was adamant that he attended. It would be good for his soul and show the locals and their peers that their son was an equal. Father was of the opposite opinion. The Catholics were the bane of society and responsible for more corruption throughout history than any other religion. They robbed, stole, and killed in the name of Jehovah, Jesus, and Mary. Any country or person that accused them of wrongdoing was either conquered and their treasure abducted, or they were unjustly imprisoned, tortured, and disposed of. No, his son had no time for organized religion. It would be his choice as to when he pursued his beliefs. They would not force it upon him.

He took his father's suggestion to heart and never once stepped foot in a church to talk with his maker. There was no time for such frivolous activities. How could an unknown entity further his education and advancement yet never once show itself? He realized now of his folly and how insignificant his accomplishments were. He would have prayed, but he knew not how or to whom.

Gough remembered the last sight he recalled were two large orbs of green and red light staring at him. They became larger and larger before the lights went out. What were they? Where had they come from? The building. Yes. He was staring at the building where all the commotion came from.

Perhaps he was not dead after all, only unconscious. But even in the conscious world, there should still be feeling, should there not? Another question he could not answer.

He felt sweat building up under his tunic and running down his legs. Wherever he was it was unusually warm, even hot. But how? If he was in Stalingrad, he should be shivering with the cold not sweating. He tried to crack a smile; he could not tell if his mouth responded. He was either on a train or plane winging back to the *fatherland*. Yes, that was it. Someone had found him; he must have been wounded. He was still recovering from his unknown wound or wounds and was still under the effects of the anesthesia. But if he was on one of those conveyances, would he not hear the wind and engines blasting through the air? Would he not smell the acrid scent of coal boiling out of the smokestack or feel the rumble of rails underneath?

There should be voices, though subtle; voices soothing him, telling him everything was going to be fine. Again, no answers to his questions.

The silence began grating on him. This is not the way for a man of his stature to depart the world. No fanfare. No bands. No medal ceremonies. No honors to bestow upon himself or his family. Nothing but this damn silence!

In his quandary of despair and self-pity, he tried the last thing he thought he would never submit to—prayer. He did not know how, but there was no better time than now. If a divine being existed, what would it hurt? And if it did not, nothing was lost.

*God or whoever you are. Send me a sign to let me know I am alive or dead. And if I am dead, let me know there is more to the afterlife than nothingness. Let me know one way or the other who was correct, my mother or father, in matters of religion and faith. If you fail to answer me, I will make my own assumptions concerning your existence.*

It was a feeble attempt at contacting the creator. There was no answer.

\* \* \*

The four took their prisoner to one of the lower levels of the chemical plant. Gough was bound up like a mummy and still in the catatonic state Dina and Svetlana had placed him in. It was an old trick they seldom used to quiet a captive. Svetlana was pleased to see her powers still worked.

"Now that we have him, what shall we do with him?" asked Svetlana.

"Kill him as if he were a stray dog," barked Otto.

"We could suck him dry then dispose of the body in a prominent area showing those who oppose us what is in store for them," answered Elizabeth.

"Or we could convert him for future use," replied Dina.

The three stared at her. "And why would we do that?" asked her sister.

"If Mother and I would have converted Colonel Eckhardt instead of sucking him dry, we might not find ourselves in such a dilemma."

"Of what use would he be to us?" asked her mother.

"One day, when you aggravated the aberration and it knocked you out, it informed me to look for allies where we least expected them."

"And?"

"Perhaps this is what she was talking about?"

"I say we kill him and gut his body then hang it from a building! That will let those German bastards know who the true master race is!" yelled Otto.

"Wait, Otto. She has a point. The old woman told me something similar. We should consider it before being hasty," said Elizabeth.

"Why?"

"Because, husband. We might not see the advantage at the moment, but I would hate to waste a valuable chip. Besides, if we do convert him, he will only be with us a short time."

"How?"

"That, husband, is where you need a lesson. Our blood was mixed with the black plague over a hundred years ago. The mixture produces a virus that when properly injected into a host, matures in ninety days and the infected superheats and melts, never to rise again."

"And who would perform the task?"

"Any three of us can do it."

Svetlana stood up. "That is not completely true. Only Dina and I can administer the change. Elizabeth's blood is not pure; there is no guarantee it would work."

The four stared at the German.

"When?" asked Elizabeth.

"In time. We need to feed first to make sure our blood levels remain high. When we do this, Dina, remember, only a pint and no more. "

"I will, Mother."

"Good. Let us go feed."

\* \* \*

When Gough awoke, he noticed his feelings and senses had returned. His consciousness returned. He could smell and feel the warmth of the fire. Yet something was off. They were intense sensations. He backed away from the fire; his skin felt as if it were burning. The bright yellows and oranges of the fire hurt his eyes. His optometrist always complimented and marveled at his perfect 20/10 eyesight. It appeared his vision had sharpened considerably.

He pushed his body back towards a wall; he detected four other beings in the room beyond the flames.

He could feel their eyes scanning him. For what, he did not know. His first instinct was to find a weapon to protect himself, but the urge passed as quickly as it appeared. The next thing he noticed was the odd sensation of thirst. It was not for water though—it was blood. His nostrils filled with the coppery scent of discarded blood. Some of it came from the four who were staring at him. It was even stronger to the left of them where three corpses were stacked. Rather than retching at the sight, he was drawn towards it.

"Dina, it looks like it took. He looks like a wolf ready to pounce on its prey."

"Yes, he does, Mother."

"Drag one over to him. Let us see what happens."

Instead of letting Dina drag the body, Otto stood up, walked over to the pile, picked one up, and threw it at Gough. "Here, you filthy pig. Feed off one of your own."

The body struck the wall with a sickening thud. Gough watched it slide down and cursed for the vital fluid that had sprayed him with the impact and felt further rage as it stuck to the walls. He took the corpse and sucked it dry.

The four looked on as he feasted.

Elizabeth watched him devour the body. "I think it is time we introduced ourselves to our new, willing comrade."

Otto agreed. The four walked over to Gough. Otto brought another half-empty corpse and threw it on his lap.

He recognized the two younger girls. The smallest is the one he saw in his sights, and the older one is the one who moved her and took the bullet. *Why isn't she dead?* He never missed.

Svetlana took the lead. "I am sure you are a little confused right now. That will pass. You are no longer of the mortal race. My daughter and I have brought you into our fold. How, is not your concern. What is of importance is you are now one of us and will do exactly as we instruct you. Your memories have not been altered; only your physiology has. You will only take and obey orders from us. The skills you possess will now be used more appropriately. You will kill without discrimination and enjoy it. You will no longer feast at a table or enjoy a fine wine. You are one of us and will endure the same hardships and perils we do. If at any time your conscience awakens and you decide to do otherwise, we will kill you. Any questions?"

Anger welled up in him as he sucked the last blood out of one of his ex-comrades. *How dare this common woman give me orders! And who are these other three fools staring at me?*

The more she talked the angrier he became. He could feel his blood surging beyond safe human limits. Yet his heartbeat was missing. An unusual sensation took over. He could detect muscles and bones moving in his arms and legs. Blood began seeping from his fingernail beds. Coarse hair started covering his hands. His eyes panned the room searching for an answer. They locked on a broken mirror.

"What in God's name am I becoming?" he growled.

Elizabeth and Otto knelt down. "One of us!."

# Chapter 21

# Panzers

The training regime was grueling. General Guttenberg did not tolerate fools, and the clans were more than amateurs; they were incompetent fumblers of which they were reminded hour by hour and day by day by the general. What shocked them more was how he and his soldiers adapted to their new forms. Those who were converted were mindless gnomes who only followed orders. Kirilli thought back to when they ambushed General von der Graff and how the converted guards only did exactly what they were told. This group behaved differently. Their motions were meticulous and exact. They never faltered or complained. The orders Guttenberg barked out were carried out and performed with expert precision.

For weeks, he met with the clans and taught them how the weapons operated: start-up, maintenance, gears, gunsight, loading, firing, electronics, hydraulics, tracks, and camouflage. Tactics was the most difficult of the lessons to learn and comprehend. When they first watched them in combat, they could not imagine how intricately a platoon and squad operated together. Each one protected the other's flank depending on the formation chosen and based on the enemy they were facing: wedge, inverted wedge, single-out, wheel, and double envelopment wedges. The terms meant nothing at first, but as the weeks progressed, they became more adept at executing the orders.

Roman embraced the training, even if it was from a convert. He did not have a long history of warfare or old tactics to cloud his mind and judgment. He threw himself into the training with a zest his mother, Konstantin, and the others could only admire. Igor was not as accommodating when it came to being ordered about by Roman and the German. His allegiance was only to Konstantin and no one else. Several times his commander was required to calm him down, reminding him of the purpose of their mission, and when the time was right, all accounts would be properly addressed.

* * *

"You idiot!" screamed Guttenberg at Igor. "Do you not know your right from your left? It is so simple. Rechts, Links. Rechts, Links. What is hard to understand about that, you incompetent Russian? What?!" He ran up to the tank, glaring at him. "When I signal left, you turn left not right, not reverse, not straight, but *left*." He held up his riding crop threatening to strike him. Before he could start the whipping, Konstantin grabbed his hand.

"Herr General. Be patient with him. He is a good man not familiar with your signals. I promise he will do better, but I also promise that if you provoke him, I will not be responsible for his actions." A touch of fire flickered in his eyes.

He lowered his crop. "Konstantin, we have been practicing the same maneuver for over a week, and he still does not understand what we are doing. Perhaps you can convince him to read the manuals and follow orders." He walked off and talked to the other crews.

Igor's face was beet red. "No one is going to address me in such a manner other than you, and even then, I might not be receptive."

"My dear friend, it is in our best interests to familiarize ourselves with these foreign machines and tactics. No, it is not what we are used to, but we must adapt. I have been in touch with Georgy and he has a special mission for us."

He cocked his head. "What is it and why can we not use our tried and true methods?"

"A good question, my friend. This is a new age of iron machines and weapons we have never seen. In order for us to keep our anonymity, we must blend in. What he is training us for is not a local action, which we excel at; we will be part of a larger force assigned to crushing the last resistance of the 6th Army, then turning east and beginning the long road back."

"I still believe we could accomplish the task without submitting to this pompous ass's abuse."

"My friend, let me remind you that Roman, Kirilli, and Sasha are outperforming you in all areas. Roman is showing the capabilities of a competent tank commander. Kirilli, a good gunner and Sasha, an efficient loader. The others are obtaining rudimentary mechanical skills." He let that sink in for a moment.

"What of you, Konstantin? What are you learning of use?"

He let out a laugh. "Tactics, Igor. Tactics. At first, like you, I saw no need for endless drills or studies. I have come to see the beauty in their movements; it is like conducting a brilliant symphony. Every instrument has a purpose, and if one is out of sync, the entire performance is a failure. Even though each unit is a separate weapon, it works in concert with the others to achieve the desired result—victory. Can you recall any army we have served or fought over the centuries that moved with such lightning speed and conquered as much territory?"

"No."

"Correct. Their tactic of blitzkrieg is a fascinating concept. I only wish we could train with the artillery, infantry, and air force to grasp the full and complete concept. Did you think an invader could destroy Poland and France in such short order, or for that matter dive this deep into our *motherland*?"

Again, he nodded no.

"Exactly, my friend. What we are learning will serve us well in the coming years and decades. Do you agree?"

Igor wiped the grim look from his face, then smiled. "Konstantin, this is why I have followed you all these years. You have an insight I will never possess, and the correct demeanor to rationalize current events. Very well, I will work harder and spend more time in study. I will not be outdone by the likes of the Boirarskys."

"That is the spirit, my friend. Keep at it, and before you know it, it will be second nature. But be quick. Time is not on our side. The general informed me we are getting low on fuel and will have to acquire some in the next few days before the tanks go dry and the engines seize up. Plus, we must become a welded fighting force in less than two weeks."

"I understand and will comply."

"Excellent, old friend. Excellent."

He walked off towards the general as Igor reacquainted himself with the steering pedals and gears.

\* \* \*

"Herr General, I believe you are about to see a noticeable change in the driver's attitude."

"Good. We are short on time and supplies and we cannot tolerate any more childish mistakes. I must take a contingent out in a few days to intercept or divert a fuel convoy to our thirsting tanks. I still have my ID papers, but I am sure my appearance could set off an alarm if recognized or at least be posed with some difficult questions to answer."

"We could take it by force."

"We could, but if any of the soldiers in the convoy are able to escape and raise an alarm, it could put our mission in jeopardy."

"Yes. I see your point. What do you suggest?"

He pulled out a sheet of paper from his inside breast pocket. "I was carrying these when we met. It is the fuel depot delivery schedule. One is scheduled tomorrow night."

"In Rostov?"

"Yes."

"I know we can ambush the train, but would it not be better to intercept the actual convoy headed to Bataysk? Plus, we would be saving fuel, would we not?"

"Excellent observation, Konstantin. I will make you a good German soldier yet."

He grimaced with the thought. "I shall make the required preparations with my people."

"And I mine. We leave tomorrow night. And Konstantin."

"Yes, General?"

"Give the men the day off tomorrow. They have earned it."

\* \* \*

Colonel Schörner and Major Hanstafnagel watched the last of the fifty trucks in the convoy cross the Don. It could not have been a better night. The cloudless sky allowed the bright luminous moon to light up the countryside as far as the eye could see, making it difficult for partisans to surprise the precious cargo they were harboring.

Von Manstein's order was specific, "Deliver the cargo on time and without fail. Loss of any of the fuel will result in harsh penalties and demotions." To ensure there were no problems, a contingent of over one hundred men was assigned to the detail. They were positioned on the flanks varying from two to three kilometers out. The vanguard swept the area two kilometers to the front, while the rearguard snugged up a kilometer behind. The Luftwaffe detailed four ME-109s for long-range reconnoitering and scouting. The chances of the partisans using aircraft were remote, but it was better to be cautious than unawares. Plus, if a threat developed, they could pounce on the intruders and either destroy them or break up the attack. The ground troops could then dispose of them at their leisure.

Schörner smiled as the last truck safely crossed the bridge. A successful mission would ensure his nomination for the Knight's Cross would go through, and with a little luck, a promotion to general would not be far behind.

"Johann."

"Jawohl, Herr Colonel."

"Any reports from the security troops?"

"Nein. All is clear."

"And the air cover?"

"Again, Herr Colonel. Nothing unusual reported."

He scanned the horizon with his binoculars. "How many times must I remind you that there is nothing unusual in this landscape. The only good thing about this route is the absence of forests where an ambush could be located. But that does not guarantee a safe trip. Ask them again. We are too close to completing our assignment."

"Jawohl, Herr Colonel."

A few minutes passed as Johann checked in with all the patrols. Schörner continued to pan the horizon, then lowered the binoculars.

"All posts report no activity."

"Excellent. One more item."

"Yes?"

"All units to understand we are not taking the highway directly to the depot. We are looping to the west and coming in from the southwest."

"Jawohl, Herr Colonel."

He sat down in the leather chair. One of the few luxuries afforded him in this hostile environment.

"Let us rejoin the convoy. We do not want to be late for our arrival, do we?"

"Nein, Herr Colonel."

Johann started up the scout car, dropped a gear, and sped off to catch the rear truck.

* * *

Konstantin, Roman, and Guttenberg watched the headlights snake across the road. Roman glanced to the sky. He could hear the buzzing of bees high above. His eyes sharpened on the flicks of blue flames coming out of exhausts.

"General. They have planes accompanying the convoy. We have never had to deal with them before."

"Correct. It is obvious the high command has made this a priority convoy. I also suspect they will have a security contingent flanking the convoy as an additional precaution to guarantee the delivery of its precious cargo. The security detail will not be a problem. But, as you pointed out, the planes do add a different dimension to the problem. Their orders will be explicit that they will not abandon the convoy until they have verification the fuel has been delivered. The only one who will have knowledge of the code words will be the officer in charge of the convoy and the commandant at the tank depot. Another dilemma we are faced with is not knowing if the tank depot will send out a scout security detail to ensure the safe delivery. We must move fast but with caution. Hasty actions will result in the entire mission and convoy being destroyed."

He pulled out a notebook, furrowed his brow, and began writing.

Konstantin and Roman continued to focus on the trucks and their path. Each minute that passed drew the trucks closer to them and their destination. They attempted to remain calm as Guttenberg continued to scribble.

He stopped writing and stared out into the darkness, watching the trucks serpentine on the road. He made one more note then stood up and stretched, gazing at the sky for a moment.

"Most inconvenient but unavoidable. This will not be an easy task, but with quick execution and an abundance of luck, I believe we can pull this off." He turned to face the two.

"Gentlemen, this is what I propose."

Konstantin and Roman read his notes.

"Are you mad?" yelled Konstantin.

"Perhaps."

\* \* \*

"Achtung! Achtung! This is Lieutenant Richter. Panzers detected at 300 meters. Is this an exercise? Repeat, is this an exercise? Confirmation required."

"Herr Colonel. You need to listen to this." He took the headset.

"Achtung! Achtung! Panzers approaching from the southeast in formation. Request confirmation. Please respond."

"Major. Raise our air cover. Have them buzz the formation and confirm identity. Notify Richter to hold position until identity is confirmed. Instruct the convoy to stop until this is sorted out. Have Lieutenant Mueller maintain his patrol on the right flank."

"Jawohl, Herr Colonel."

\* \* \*

Guttenberg rode high in the cupola of his PzKpfw IV watching the planes and security detail closing in as he watched through his binoculars. He remained calm leading the squad to their prey. He set the squad up in a typical wedge formation, changing direction every fifty meters. It was a normal training move to teach new recruits the importance of directional changes to confuse planes and artillery observers for range finding, while ensuring the integrity of the formation's firepower remained intact.

The challenge was infiltrating the security force and disarming them without firing a shot. He still was not sure this could be accomplished, but it was the only option available. The tanks he brought held the last of the fuel reserves. If the mission failed, there would be no more training exercises, and future operations would be severely hindered.

He knew his plan was solid based on the scanty information at hand. Convincing Konstantin and Roman had been more of a challenge than he anticipated. They were not sold on the idea of using the tanks. But why would they? They did not have his experience in tactics nor seen the vehicles in a combat situation. They vied for a headlong attack using their tried and true methods. He argued, convincingly, how their methods would only raise alarms at the depot and result in failure. They were to use finesse and guile. He outlined how the clans would be the ground troops supporting the armor.

The planes would see the German battle flags identifying them as friendlies. Since they would have the correct frequencies to communicate with the convoy, they would radio to the commander that all was clear. He would then lead his tanks into the detail and calm the commander, locate the wireless, and either disable it or use it. With that accomplished, the clans would have to strike fast and hard, eliminating and replacing the detail.

They would then turn their attention to the convoy. Half of his contingent would deal with the fuel, the other the right flank force.

\* \* \*

"Repeat. This is Lieutenant Richter speaking for Colonel Schörner. Identify yourself immediately. Repeat. Respond immediately or be fired upon."

The static pouring out of the speaker was deafening. A scratchy voice filled the silence.

"This is General Guttenberg."

Schörner grabbed the headset. "General. This is Colonel Schörner of the 2$^{nd}$ Battalion, 4$^{th}$ Panzer Army. It was our understanding you and your contingency were killed or captured a few weeks back. Please explain your miraculous appearance."

"Colonel. It is true we were attacked by partisans. Many of my men were killed or wounded. Those of us who were captured were able to overcome our adversaries and are bringing them back to Rostov for justice. Their trials will be a signal to all who resist the Third Reich that resistance is futile, and their impertinence will be rewarded at the end of a rope or a bullet to the head. Heil Hitler!"

Schörner studied his comment for a moment. "Lieutenant. Raise our air cover and verify the general is leading the group. We cannot afford any mistakes."

"Jawohl, Herr Colonel."

"General. It is good to know you are in good health and will be joining your comrades in arms for our victorious push on Stalingrad. For the moment, however, please hold your position so we may identify your claim."

"I appreciate your caution, Colonel. We shall comply with the order."

Guttenberg held up his hand and the column stopped. He called out to Konstantin. "Pass the word. When the planes fly over, smile, and wave. When they realize we are friendlies, we will be allowed to approach and complete the mission."

"What if the planes do not leave?"

"It is a calculated risk. If they follow procedure, they will be instructed to fly ahead to make sure the remainder of the road is clear of obstacles and partisans. They will then return to their base of origin."

"How can you be so sure?"

"I cannot. But there is no alternative. Now, stop haggling with me and carry out my order!"

* * *

"Eagle-One, this is Vulture. What do you see?"

The BF-109s buzzed the convoy twice. Each time the men waved, cheered, and smiled as they flew over. "Eagle-One. Identify friendly forces in convoy. General is in lead tank, over."

"Eagle-One. Do you detect any unusual activity?'

"Negative, Vulture. All appears to be in order."

"Eagle-One. Proceed with assignment."

"Eagle-One to Vulture. Acknowledged."

* * *

Konstantin and Guttenberg continued waving as the planes wagged their wings and sped off to the east.

"General Guttenberg. This is Colonel Schörner. You are authorized to proceed forward and join our convoy. Welcome back, General."

"Thank you, Colonel. We are proceeding as planned, and I look forward to toasting our upcoming victory with you and your staff tonight. Heil Hitler!"

"Heil Hitler!"

* * *

The two convoys approached each other, still showing caution. Guttenberg rode high in the cupola of his tank, while the colonel stood in his Kübelwagon. One hand holding his binoculars, another clutching the fall bar.

Schörner could not have his vital mission fail. Despite the calming conversation he and the general exchanged, he detected something off in the general's voice. He had met him five years ago in Berlin during a seminar Guderian, Halder, and Hausser held on explaining the new tactic of "Blitzkrieg." His voice was smoother, deeper, and confident. Today, it was choppy, higher pitched but still confident. Perhaps his time on the frontlines had altered him. Or, the change in tone was a direct result of his captors beating him. If the latter were the case, he would look forward to personally handling the inquiries of his captors and meting out the appropriate punishment.

He instructed his driver to slow down as his vehicle and the general's tank approached each other.

He was impressed with the perfect wedge formation and the perfect spacing of the troops protecting the flanks. Guderian would be proud.

The two vehicles stopped. Schörner dismounted, straightened his tunic, and walked towards the general. Major Hanstafnagel accompanied him.

Guttenberg climbed down from the tank, straightened his cap, brushed his tunic, and waited for the colonel to approach. He raised his hand signaling for all engines to be shut down.

The only sounds were the crunching of Schörner and Hanstafnagel's boots on the frozen ground and the sound of dry branches crackling.

They came to rest three meters from the general. "Heil Hitler." They called out. Guttenberg did not return the hail.

"Herr General. It is customary for a German officer to return my greeting." The general stared straight through him. The hairs on Schörner's neck began tingling. A heaviness began engulfing the air as if a fog were rising.

One by one, he noticed the members of the platoon moving behind the general. Some were in uniforms, some were not. He also detected women in the group. He took a step back placing his hand on his revolver holster. A bead of sweat ran down his right temple.

"Herr General. I insist you explain what is going on here, immediately, or my men and I will be forced to open fire." He flipped the leather latch on his holster open.

Sounds of gunfire erupted to the south. He could see the flashes of fire then nothing.

"Major. Raise the escort group. Find out what is happening over there."

"Jawohl, Herr Colonel."

"That will not be necessary, Herr Colonel." Schörner looked up at the general. He blinked several times to make sure what he saw was in focus. Guttenberg's eyes were glowing a dark blue. He detected flashes of light coming out of them. What concerned him the most were his teeth. His incisors were at least a centimeter long and growing.

"Herr General. It appears you are sick. We need to get you to the infirmary immediately. It appears you contracted a filthy Russian disease that requires medical attention."

The general glared at him. "Colonel…." His voice was getting harsher and more garbled with each word. "That will not be necessary. I have never been in better shape."

The cracking of branches became louder. Schörner began glancing at the men and women from the tank platoon. All of their uniforms were dancing under their clothing. He removed his Luger in panic.

"General. For the last time, I demand to know what is going on here. I have a vital mission to accomplish and you are holding it up!"

"Herr Colonel..." he took a step towards him, "you have served the *fatherland* well." He took another step forward as did his comrades. "In honor of your service, I can assure you, your efforts have been noted." He took another step forward. Schörner's eyes were locked on Guttenberg's. He tried to raise his pistol in protest and self-preservation but could not. He tried to speak but could not. The general's hypnotic eyes were paralyzing him.

Guttenberg motioned for his platoon to begin spreading out.

"Herr Colonel, today you will taste, or shall I say, we shall taste, the fruits of our labors and training. But first you have one last task to perform."

Schörner forced out, "And what would that be, Herr General."

"Your life!"

\* \* \*

It was over in less than ten seconds. The entire convoy's complement was eliminated without a shot being fired. The bodies they feasted on were thrown in the back of the trucks for later disposal. Those converted remained at their assigned posts. In a few minutes, Kirilli, Igor, and Sasha joined the rest with their captured vehicles.

General Guttenberg proudly looked over his handiwork, displaying a smile. He turned and addressed the clan. "Never in all my years of military duty have I witnessed a most successful strike. Let us retire and continue our training for the next mission." He headed back to his command tank, erect and proud.

Igor, Konstantin, Roman, Kirilli, and Sasha watched him mount his vehicle. "Did you not hear me? Are you all deaf? I said it is time to retire and continue your training, *now*!" His tank swung to the right and began moving to the southeast.

Igor looked at Konstantin. "I am going to kill that German swine."

"Not unless I do it first," replied Kirilli.

"None of you will touch him until we have learned everything we can from him," answered Roman. "We need him for at least another month or so, and if any harm comes to him, I shall personally deal with that individual myself. Now, do as he says!"

They both looked at Kirilli. "We are starting to hate him just as much."

"Meaning what?"

"Meaning this; he needs to remember what clan he belongs to. Understood?" said Konstantin.

Sasha had heard enough. "If any of you are thinking about harming my son, you will answer to me. I suggest you watch your tongues and do as he says. For the moment, he is leading us, unlike you three. If he becomes too unbearable, I will handle it and only I. Until that time, let us enjoy our victory and return to our camp."

The men stood silent as she walked away.

Konstantin broke the silence with his deep, hearty laugh. "Damn, Kirilli. You should have warned us about her temper. How have you been able to corral her all these years?"

"I do not know, but before this is over, I might have to adjust her attitude."

"Good luck with that, my friend. Now, let us do as they say and return home. It has been a most successful yet trying day."

# Chapter 22

# Bezpieczeństwo

It took four days for Nicole and Dmitri to arrive home. It was a perilous journey fraught with difficulties, but the specter they encountered assured them they would pass the test. It just did not say what condition they would be in.

The castle yard was overgrown with weeds from neglect. Dmitri felt it best to leave as is so as not to attract unwanted attention. He was pleased to see vandals and homeless were not camped out at the castle. There were signs of minor theft in some of the rooms, but nothing that would raise alarm.

Nicole went to the chamber room where they had mated and fell on the dusty bed with the twins. "Dmitri. I need food. But first, could you light the fire for some warmth? I am so cold."

If he lit the hearth, the smoke would alert others the house was inhabited. He looked at the candles still in their holders and the chandelier. He knew it would take longer to warm the vast room, but it would be better that way.

Dmitri walked into several other rooms gathering all the bedding he could find. He came back, covering her and the twins. Billows of dust wafted off each blanket he fluffed and then placed on her and the boys, adding to the stale, musty air in the room. Cleaning would have to wait. The box of matches was still on the mantle over the fireplace. He struck one, making sure moisture had not ruined them. It lit! The next hours were spent lighting all the candles and making sure Nicole and the children were comfortable. Satisfied with his work, he went out to the back courtyard, staring at the altar still in place where Stephan was cremated.

A strong wind blew in from the south. Yet the limbs of the trees were bending to the south. *How can that be?*

An unmistakable voice broke his concentration. *An old enemy of the family will visit you soon. Do not treat him as an enemy. He is now an ally. Hear him out and decide the best course of action.*

The wind stopped.

\* \* \*

Nikoli went through his notes for the umpteenth time, trying to figure out how to execute his plan on the camp. Even Schmidt was perplexed with the enormity of the task at hand.

"Nikoli. Where are we going to find people to help us with this? My limited military training is not up to the scope of this operation. We would need at least a hundred heavily armed men to pull this off. We alone cannot convert that many. It would take years, and even then the rate of attrition would make the task mind-numbing."

"You are correct, my friend. Even if I could ask Konstantin and Kirilli for forgiveness and bring us back as a united clan, I doubt we could pull this off."

"You would consider trying to apologize for your past actions to the likes of them?"

Nikoli pushed his papers around the table, thinking. "Yes. Odd as it sounds, I have learned much over the past few years. I have learned humility and understanding. In the past, I was a man of steel. Any man, woman, or vampire who stood in my way would be disposed of or wear the scars of our encounter. That persona began cracking when my son Stephan was wounded by the SS during interrogation, and my wife had to finish him off. Up until then, emotions were foreign to me. I could not care less what people felt or how much pain I inflicted on them. His death caused me to rethink my mission. When I found out Svetlana betrayed me, those old feelings came back and I banished her. That, I regret. In time, I understood her motives, and I believe I would have done the same thing. I did not realize how much I depended on her advice and judgment. Of course, I would never admit agreement to her openly, but that has changed." He rose from his chair and walked to the door. "Schmidt, it is time to start making amends for the past and concentrate on the future. My intuition tells me we shall all be together again. When and how? I cannot say. But mark my words, we shall unite, forge a plan, and free those the Germans are senselessly sending to slaughter." He walked out.

The night air was crisp and clean. Nothing like the foul air that permeated his nostrils and skin at the camp. Each breath he took was the souls of those being incinerated. The thought nauseated him. *They must be freed at all costs.*

As he stood gathering his thoughts, a strong wind blew up from the south.

*Go to Bezpieczeństwo.*

## Chapter 23

## Collapse

### Univermag

The sounds of exploding shells were once a sound von Paulus cherished. They trumpeted in another victory for the mighty armies of the Third Reich as they crashed through Poland, the Lowlands, France, and Russia. The explosions signaled another glorious victory for the *fatherland*. His brave soldiers would be showered with ribbons and medals. The papers would be filled with their victorious faces. Women lined the streets cheering in anticipation of meeting the heroes who were cleansing the world of Germany's enemies. It seemed so long ago. What he heard now signaled the destruction of his once-proud 6$^{th}$ Army. For months, they surged across the Russian steppe knowing nothing but complete and total victory; in the south, the massive oil refinery at Maykop had fallen, and the troops were at the foothills of the Caucasus Mountains. Now, the defeat of his army was only weeks away. The counteroffensive to free his men came up twenty kilometers short. He watched the flashes of battle dimming farther and farther away until there was nothing to see or hear.

It was time to take stock of what options were still available to him; continue to fight, wasting his men, or surrender in the hopes they would be treated fairly. He knew the second was not an option. His interrogations of Russian prisoners revealed how Himmler's Einsatzgruppen were treating the conquered populace. The thought sickened him. To protest would go nowhere. He would be told not to worry about issues that did not affect the battlefield. If he persisted, he would be reassigned. Thus, there was only one option—continue fighting. His shoulders slumped as another Russian barrage of "Stalin Organs" erupted, showering him with dust and plaster.

* * *

## Southern Pocket

Albert and Derrick cowered under the rubble along with what was left of their company as the "Stalin Organs" continued to smash their positions. The shelling they were used to, but the sound of the rockets still unnerved them. Regular artillery shells whined as they approached, giving the defender a good idea where it might land. The organs did not. They made a sound like screaming banshees descending on them, never knowing where they were going to land. They instinctively ducked as the salvo fell and exploded.

"Albert. Do you think we will ever see our homeland again?"

"Nein."

"Why do you say that?"

"When was the last time our bellies were full? When was the last time we were able to properly bathe? When was the last supply of ammunition received? Our only supply line is our dead and fallen comrades. What does that tell you, Derrick?"

"Perhaps the supply trucks are having difficulty navigating the debris-strewn streets, or maybe our brave forces at Gumrak are fighting off another counterattack. I will not believe our Führer has forgotten us."

"My poor Albert. It is good to see you still have faith in our leader. The reality of our situation is simple; we have been abandoned to tie up as many Russian forces as possible so our generals can stabilize the front and slow down the Russians. For us, it is only a matter of time before we are captured or die. Those are the facts."

"Then there is still hope for us."

"I tire of debating with you. There has been no hope for us since the middle of December. Herr Meyer Goering swore he would keep us supplied. He failed. I will say it one more time. We have been abandoned, and no one is coming to rescue any of us. Now, shut up and let me get some rest before the hordes come at us."

Albert removed his pistol and aimed it at Derrick. "You are, and those like you, are the reason we lost this battle. Your defeatist attitude spread through the ranks poisoning too many minds. If you would have kept your mind clean and clear and thought only of final victory, we would have captured Stalingrad months ago, and been home lying with our wives and girlfriends instead of hiding like rats in this hollowed-out city. Therefore, it is my duty to…"

"To what?" he saw him raising the pistol.

"To eliminate our ranks of dissenters such as…"

He never saw the knife Derrick was holding until it plunged into his stomach.

"You should not have done that," came an unfamiliar voice.

"And why not?"

"Because we only feast on live, warm blood."

\* \* \*

Garron, Berg, and Fritz were grizzled veterans of three years. They served together in Poland, France, and now Russia. Death came with the job. The carnage they witnessed in Warsaw unnerved them at first. Death was only a word they knew by definition. Seeing it face-to-face was another issue. They made the mistake of eating lunch before touring the conquered city. They were not ready for the sights of disemboweled and shattered bodies. All their lunches were left on the streets of Warsaw.

The years hardened them as death became a daily occurrence. Looking away when a comrade was hit did not turn their stomachs; they did what they could for them before the medics arrived. If they were too far gone, they helped themselves to their departed comrade's equipment he no longer needed.

But Stalingrad was a whole new terror. It resembled something from a Grimm's fairy tale, only worse. They were never in a town or city that smelled and felt of death at every corner like Stalingrad. No matter where you went, there were bodies. Some complete, others partially intact. If he looked hard enough, fragments of men were everywhere. This created a feeding frenzy for the rats of the city. Many times, they and the Russians would take up the sport of killing the rats rather than each other. The thought of their brethren being eaten was too much for both sides. When time permitted and officers were not looking, they would have a contest and yell out outrageous claims. It helped ease the madness.

Today was different. The Russians were squeezing them back to the Volga, meter by meter. They were forced to leave their wounded behind in hopes they would receive proper medical care; they were mistaken.

The three were the rearguard for the company and took up a position one hundred meters from the makeshift hospital to observe and report. Three T-34s with about thirty men came into view. The recon squad stopped and surveyed the hospital; an officer walked among the wounded for a few minutes. Instead of having his men check the wounded, he gave the signal for the tanks to move forward. The sight of watching the bodies of their comrades exploding, spreading blood, guts, and bone on the advancing troops hit a nerve. One of the tankers was having too much fun. It would advance a few meters, then do a 360 on the bodies. The screams of the wounded penetrated their souls igniting an anger they had never felt before. The three looked at each other, loaded their weapons, took their last drink of water, then rushed out to avenge the fallen.

## Northern Pocket

*How could this happen?* thought Colonel Werner. He joined the Wehrmacht in 1935 as a lowly private looking for adventure and a way out of the rampant poverty that plagued his vaunted *fatherland*. He was raised by his father and mother to hate the French and the British for the horrible Versailles Treaty forced upon Germany at the conclusion of World War I. The reparations levied on the country, along with the financial collapse of 1929, left this once-proud country the laughingstock and whipping boy of the capitalist conquerors.

He watched his parents struggle daily to keep their four children fed at least once a day and keep a roof over their heads. Father worked whatever job he could find, and Mother tailored items for neighbors to supplement their meager earnings.

That began to change in 1933 with the rise of Adolf Hitler and his National Socialist Worker's Party. Hitler promised a new and stronger Germany would rise out of the ashes and repay those who had tried to grind her into dust and eliminate the name of Germany from the history books. Those countries became richer and more pompous while they bled his country dry. Hitler's Third Reich would endure for a thousand years, and those that stood in the way would be eliminated. Hitler scrapped the Versailles Treaty and its ridiculous mandate that Germany's army could only number one hundred thousand, and they were not allowed to have an air force. What nonsense!

He and his brothers and sisters would be transfixed when their father sat and talked of his glorious times as a young captain in the trenches in the Argonne, Ypres, and Belleau Wood. They could envision his brave men battling the French, English, and Americans in a just cause. The country went to war to ensure its rightful place in the world order. They were only protecting their interests and fighting off those who wanted to pillage and plunder their proud country. It was now his time to follow in the footsteps of his father.

Within a year, his sergeant recognized young Alexander's propensity for correctly diagnosing complicated military exercises and executing orders to the T. He was never insolent when given an impossible order to carry out. He would suggest a different line of attack with great zeal. Many times, his sergeant was amazed at the boy's grasp of difficult situations and his ability to predict the outcomes. He was nominated to attend the General Staff College. Alexander passed the entrance exam with ease excelling in mathematics, logistics, and organization. In less than two years he graduated as a first lieutenant. His instructors saw no reason for him to start at the bottom as a second lieutenant.

His father and mother beamed at his graduation in the fall of 1937. They were personally invited to sit in the reviewing stand with Adolf, Heinrich Himmler, and Hermann Goering!

They watched their son lead his training class through the parade ground, smartly executing the goose-step march with their right arms raised high ushering in the new Germany.

In 1939, he found himself attached to Guderian's XIX Corps. The victory was swift and flawless. His bravery on the front earned him the Iron Cross First Class, the Wound Badge, and a promotion to captain. He recovered from his injury in time to be assigned to Rommel's 7th Panzer Division. He was given the command of a squad of PzKwIIIs, with support from two Sturmgeschütz assault guns and a battalion of infantry. His commanding officers were not sure about placing a young officer with such a weighty assignment. Their commander, Erwin Rommel, calmed their fears. He proudly led his victorious contingent into Arras and unto Dunkirk. While his performance exceeded all expectations, he was furious that his unit was ordered to halt and reorganize on May 24th. He knew they were on the cusp of a great victory with the BEF bottled up on the coast around Dunkirk. He was convinced his men could run to the coast then knife down to the south, cutting off any type of escape route. Werner voiced his concerns to his superiors. They sympathized with his analysis, but when he received a reply to his protestation from Rommel that the action was authorized by the Führer, he withdrew his complaints and followed the order.

His actions in France earned him the German Gold Cross, Tank Battle Badge, a promotion to major, and a thirty-day leave. It was a glorious time!

Upon his arrival in Magdeburg, a throng of people greeted him at the train station. Everyone wanted to meet and welcome the hero of the Reich for his glorious accomplishments. He was overwhelmed by the reception. Tears welled up when he disembarked the train and saw his father standing erect, with his mother and his sibling saluting him. For the next twenty-five days, he wanted for nothing. Every night was filled with wine, fine dining, and any woman he chose. It was definitely a hero's welcome.

He would regale his listeners with his glorious exploits of swatting down the Poles as if they were nothing but a nuisance. He described them as an annoying fly that needed to be swatted down. This would bring howling laughter from his enraptured crowd. He was not much kinder to the British or French forces. He would describe them as large armies with no direction or leadership. The only thing you could count on with them was the time they had their tea or required rest, even though they had accomplished nothing in a day's work. His mesmerized audiences were fascinated with his descriptions of the new panzer divisions and how fast they moved and cut through the enemy lines like a hot knife through butter.

With the end of exciting, heroic tales, they boisterously applauded his adventures, convinced winning the war was only months away. With men like Major Alexander Werner leading their brave soldiers, who could stand up to them?

He, like many, was convinced there was no other country to conquer. Goebbels filled the airwaves and papers with glorious propaganda. Even though Goering was not able to knock out England in 1940, Doenitz and his U-boats would sever their supply lines and force Britain to capitulate. North Africa and the Middle East would be conquered and annexed within a year. With those countries under the protection of the new Germany, there would be no one left to fight. So he thought.

When he returned to his unit, he was notified they were being transferred to Eastern Poland. His unit was being assigned to the 2$^{nd}$ Panzer Group under his old mentor Guderian. Then he heard the rumor—their ally, the Soviet Union, was next on Hitler's list. When he attended the staff meeting laying out Operation *Barbarossa*, it was the first time he questioned his leader's goals and objectives. This was not a small task. He was enthralled with the scope of the operation. Army Group North under General von Leeb would strike north and take Leningrad. His unit would be part of Army Group Centre striking to Moscow, and Army South would drive on the Ukraine capturing Sevastopol.

The scope was a massive undertaking. The Soviet Union did not have an advanced road network, and the Russian rail was of a different gauge. The engineering units would have their hands full keeping the front-line units supplied.

The plan called for all objectives to be reached before or shortly after the *Rasputitsa* hit. Other than that, they should run into only minor difficulties and sporadic resistance. It was believed the Russian army was a house of cards, and once the glorious panzer divisions broke through the front lines, the entire country would collapse, and Stalin would be forced to negotiate a surrender treaty.

On June 22nd, the invasion began. At first, they were met with limited resistance. The plan was moving forward with German precision. The Russians were fleeing and dying by the tens of thousands. The Luftwaffe destroyed the bulk of the pathetic Russian Air Force in less than a week. There was nothing to stop them.

His unit was part of the encirclement and victories at Smolensk and Kiev. They captured over seven hundred thousand Russians and untold amounts of equipment and material. For his achievements during those battles, he was awarded the Knight's Cross and promotion to lieutenant colonel. He marveled at his meteoric rise in the ranks. In six short years, he was two steps from becoming one of the youngest generals in the Wehrmacht. This vision was reinforced when Hitler placed the Ritterkreuzträger around his neck. Leaning in, he whispered, "I need men like you on my General Staff. You are the lifeblood Germany is fighting for."

What he was not aware of was that as he was being presented with the award, his comrades were reeling back from the gates of Moscow. The Russians were not finished fighting. Von Leeb had not taken Leningrad, nor had Sevastopol fallen.

After the ceremony, he went home for two weeks. The gaiety he left less than six months ago was dissipating. While the townsfolk greeted him enthusiastically, the mood at the hofbrau was more subdued. The British had begun bombing their cities at night with rapidity, and there was talk of America coming into the conflict on Britain and Russia's side. Despite the rumors, Goebbels' propaganda machine was working in full force declaring Germany was on the cusp of the greatest victory in all of history. Germany would not only conquer Russia, but eliminate communism and cleanse the country for German farmers and settlers. Werner was still convinced that with the right plan and leadership, 1942 would be the end of the war. North Africa and the Middle East would be theirs. Then they would knock out England, lessening the effect of the United States entering the war.

His unit was assigned to von Paulus's 6th Army. Their mission was to seize Sevastopol, Rostov-on-Don, drive to the Caucasus Mountains, and meet up with Rommel's Afrika Korps. Stalingrad would be sealed off and starved out.

Case Blau jumped off on June 28th, 1942. The start of the offensive came with a promotion to full colonel. One step closer to the high command.

Sevastopol fell. Rostov-on-Don fell. The troops were driving on the Caucasus Mountains, and his unit was going to Stalingrad and final victory!

In less than two months, the tables were turned. Instead of final victory, the 6th Army was trapped, and Army Group A was dashing back to Rostov to avoid being cut off and annihilated.

*How had this happened? What had gone wrong? Who was to blame?* Those thoughts consumed him as he finished reading the letter he received from his aunt. His father, mother, and sister were killed a month ago during an air raid. His oldest brother Victor was missing in action around Leningrad, and his younger brother was assumed dead in North Africa. Tears flowed freely as the anger and rage surfaced to the top. He felt as his father did—they, the German people, had been deceived and lied to by the leaders they supported. They were responsible for the inglorious surrender in November of 1918, and now they were responsible for the current defeats. Liars, betrayers, deceivers! They, Hitler, Himmler, Goebbels, Goering, and Keitel sat in their safe havens issuing nonsensical orders, spouting unheeded propaganda that would change nothing other than guarantee the elimination of more lives. He wondered many times what the animals in cages at the Berlin Zoo felt like. He now knew—trapped! But at least the animals were fed. It had been three weeks since he enjoyed a hot meal with meat. He and his men were lucky to receive a half of a cold potato. Another blast of artillery rounds falling shook him out of his stupor. It also woke up the lice that infested his dirty, torn tunic. At least *they* were not starving.

Each salvo that exploded rained down more dirt and dust in the improvised bunker. His last surviving officer, Lieutenant Wagner, fell through the burlap covering.

"Colonel. What are your orders?"

"In regards to what, Lieutenant?"

"Repelling the Russians, Herr Colonel?"

"How many men are left? How much ammunition does each carry? What is their morale?"

"We have twenty able-bodied men. Enough ammunition for two days. Morale is high. The men believe it is only a matter of time before we are relieved."

Werner stared at the idealistic lieutenant. Everything he just said was a lie. He learned through the years to check on his men periodically to make sure of their readiness and worthiness in combat. While the lieutenant slept during his assigned post last night, Werner reconnoitered his position for his own satisfaction. Of the forty men left in his command, twenty were frozen, he sent ten to the makeshift hospital, five were missing, leaving only five to command. They each had fifteen rounds apiece for their rifles of which only two were operational. When he looked in their eyes, he saw nothing but hopelessness. He would have much rather seen the fear they displayed not but a month ago.

He slid his hand down, unlocking his holster. "Lieutenant, you have served our Führer and the Reich exemplarily under these severe conditions. I would like you to know, I have put you in for the Iron Cross First Class and a promotion to captain. The Third Reich needs more brave men like you."

The lieutenant stood tall, clicked his worn, snow-covered boots, and howled out, "Thank you, Herr Colonel. Heil Hitler."

Werner stood up, returned the salute, and put a bullet between the lieutenant's eyes.

"Heil Hitler."

A salvo of "Stalin Organs" rained down on the bunker.

\* \* \*

The story was the same around the tightening noose. One by one, the pockets of resistance went silent. Zhukov, Chuikov, and Khrushchev knew the end was near. Several attempts were made to von Paulus to surrender his beleaguered force. He refused. If they would not surrender, then the only action left was to grind the enemy into the ruins, and let him know that it was he who brought death and despair to his people and that his leaders had abandoned him.

Day by day, the Russian forces squeezed the pocket smaller and smaller. Khrushchev laughed to himself as he squeezed the last drop of an orange into his vodka. "Just like the Germans. When we are finished, there will not be enough of them to fertilize our fields." He discarded the rind on the muddy floor, then stomped on it with his heavy boot, expelling the remaining drops.

# Chapter 24

# Abandoned

**January 5th, 1943**
**Univermag**

Von Paulus slammed the phone down.

"Bad news, Herr General?"

"What do you think, Major?'

"By your actions, it is not good."

"Very observant, Wilhelm. Very observant. That madman in Berlin still thinks we can win this battle. He is convinced the Russians are at the end of their rope, and this is nothing BUT a last-ditch effort from them. They have reached the bottom of the barrel and will be defeated."

"And you disagree with the Führer?"

"Of course, I do. But I am not ignorant enough to voice that opinion, not that it would matter. It is only a matter of time now."

"Until what, Herr General?"

"Good Lord, Wilhelm. Must I explain in detail what is going on? Have you forgotten how to read a map? This battle was lost in December when General Manstein's Operation *Wintergewitter* failed. That, coupled with Goering's boast he could supply the requisite seven hundred tonnes of supplies a day, and at best, we only receive two hundred, is evidence we are going to lose this battle."

"General, I would like to think that our Führer is building up the required forces for a break-out to be successful. They would not abandon us. And, we have never lost a battle before. I cannot and will not believe what you are saying. It is defeatist talk, which borders on insubordination and a charge of court-martial."

"Wilhelm, believe what you wish. Tell me though, what forces are going to materialize and break through the Russians? Army Group A has retreated from the Caucasus Mountains and is hanging on to Rostov with their fingernails. It is only a matter of time before they are pushed back to Sevastopol. Perhaps help will come from our forces around Moscow? That too is doubtful. They are still licking their wounds and rebuilding after the failed attempt to capture the capitol in '41. Maybe Rommel's Afrika Korps will be our savior? That too is a pipe dream. He has his hands full with the British right now. He is advancing towards Cairo, but by the time he takes it and conquers the Middle East, we will all be long gone. No, Wilhelm, there is no hope for us. We are like grapes on the vine when the first frosts hits—undesirable and useless. Even the birds will not give us a second look for scavenging. We will rot on the ground and be trampled and plowed upon when it is time for the next planting season. No, Wilhelm, our fate is sealed."

"But why, Herr General? Why would Berlin abandon us in our time of need?"

"According to Hitler, we are serving a glorious function for the Third Reich by tying up over a million Russians who could be used on other fronts."

"But is it not true? We *are* tying down Russian forces."

"Enough of your insufferable views. We are not tying down anything. The Russians continue to expand the outer rings while crushing the life out of my army. That, Wilhelm, is our reality. There is no relief force coming. There will be no miracle in the east. Whether it is this month or the next, we are all going to perish in this shell of a city. At one time, I believed victory was in our grasp. Time, distance, weather, and partisans have been our undoing. We should have solidified our axis: Rostov-Stalingrad-Moscow-Leningrad. With that line intact, then we could look to the south and the oilfields instead of dashing into the unknown.

Even though they will not admit it, OKH severely underestimated the resilience and capacity of the Russians to fill their depleted ranks and continue to build the implements of war. Add the aid from America to the equation and, my dear Wilhelm, it is a recipe for disaster."

"Then what orders do you have for the troops if all is lost?"

"If you have to ask, then you know nothing of soldiering and I should send you to the front lines, for at this time, I have no use of an aide. No matter the situation, a soldier must carry out the one order he knows—fight. Now, leave me. I tire of this pointless discussion."

"Jawohl, Herr General."

"And Wilhelm."

"Yes, Herr General."

"I remand the suggestion of you going to the front. You will not have to go to it. It is coming for us both."

\* \* \*

Zhukov and Stalin could not have been more pleased with themselves. Operation *Little Saturn,* coupled with the prior success of Operation *Uranus,* had entrapped the vaunted 6th Army, stopped the relief effort, forced Army Group A out of the Caucasus Mountains, and was in the process of reclaiming the rich, fertile lands of the Ukraine. The tide was turned. The once-invincible armies of the Third Reich were faltering. Unlike their opponent, they could not replace the men and materials they were losing at an alarming rate.

Stalin slapped his favorite general on the back. "Georgy We should drink a toast to victory. At our current pace, we should be knocking on Hitler's door in less than a year. Come, let's drink."

"Comrade Stalin, at this time I shall pass. There is much work to do, and I doubt the war will be over in a year.

Leningrad is still surrounded, and they still threaten Moscow. No, Comrade Stalin, I will not drink until my soldiers can share the drink with us."

"General, you are too cautious. The writing is on the wall. It is only a matter of time."

"Comrade Stalin, it is my caution that has allowed us to deal these blows to the Germans. Based on current reports, the army is at the end of its advance. They are running low on ammunition, men, and supplies. They need to regroup and refit before our next move."

"Nonsense, Georgy. I am confident they will retake Kharkov and keep pushing the fascists out of our *motherland*!"

"Such a move at this time will expose our weak units to a counterattack of which I do not believe they would be able to repulse. I prefer to stop now and prepare for the spring offenses when our forces are replenished and rested."

Stalin slammed his fist on the map.

"I am ordering you to take Kharkov immediately!"

"Yes, Comrade Stalin. Remember, if the battle fails, you have only yourself to blame."

He furrowed his brow as his face turned beet red. He glanced at the map one more time then began relaxing.

"Very well, Georgy. Do what you can but still, we should honor our heroes of the Soviet Union with a toast. Please, join me this once. We will not drink again until the enemy has been thrown off our soil and the sound of guns are heard in Berlin. Agreed?"

"Agreed, Comrade Stalin."

## Chapter 25

## Nikoli

Nikoli called the remnants of his clan together: Yakov, Taras, Natashia, and Schmidt. They came into the poorly lit, drafty room and took their respective seats, wondering why he wanted to talk. During his absence, they enjoyed doing what they wanted and hunting when they chose while not being under his rule. They even made a few minor improvements to the compound for their own comfort. Yakov and Natashia were not enthused when Nikoli returned. They were enjoying the newfound freedoms without their master being around to spoil their forays. Now he was back. They agreed that if he tried to pick up where he left off, they would join forces and evict him forever from Tarnow. It was now their home, not his, and they would not hesitate to fight him for it.

So far, he had displayed none of his prior bombastic, overbearing traits.

\* \* \*

Nikoli spent an hour reminiscing and mourning the loss of his son. The cold wind whipped around him as he recalled that fateful night at Gestapo headquarters. At the time, he chalked it up to an acceptable battle loss. The last years of fighting and strife were changing his attitudes. He realized times were changing, and his past tactics were no longer relevant. If he wished to survive the modern age, he would also have to change and adjust.

As he walked down the hall to the meeting room, he stopped and glanced at the painting he brought home for

Svetlana. The sight of the waves crashing against the rocks was an excellent description of his past actions. He could not decide if he was the waves trying to destroy the rocks or the opposite. He could see himself as both. The waves were him beating down his foes, forcing his will on others, while the rocks were him standing up to resistance. Or was it? Yes, in the past he took everything by force and iron will, including Svetlana. It was that thinking that had split the clans and found him on the outside. His days of a harsh rule were over. If there were any hope of carrying out his lofty plan, he would have to change. He walked into the room with an odd recurring thought, *Svetlana, I miss you. Forgive me.*

* * *

He took his place and sat down.
"Thank you for coming. The old ways of conducting business are over. It is time for a change, and it starts with me. Since my absence, much has changed."
"Yes, it has," Natashia muttered.
"I realize I have no right coming back here and giving orders or eliciting your help."
Again, Natashia replied, only louder. "Again, you are correct."
"Natashia, let him finish. I am curious where this is going." Replied Yakov.
"Why? You know how he is and how he treated us in the past. He is only concerned with his own hide at whatever cost."
"Perhaps. But still, I detect a slight change in his demeanor. Let him continue without any more interruptions."
Nikoli stood up. "Natashia, you have every right to detest me. I was an overbearing ogre who, as you so aptly pointed out, cared nothing but of my own wants and desires.

Trust me. That attitude is gone. I have lost a son, a daughter to the melding, my wife, and also my brother."

This took them all by shock. "Konstantin banished you?" asked Yakov.

"Yes. Along with Kirilli and Roman. They have replaced me."

"For what reason? I never thought you and Konstantin could be separated."

"For the same reasons Natashia mentioned. My arrogance has cost me everything. As I was saying, it is time for me to change and that has already happened. I am learning how to compromise and listen to the opinions of others. I am more flexible when it comes to differing views and tactics. If you are not convinced, ask my friend, Corporal Schmidt. I believe he will vouch for my statements."

Yakov contemplated the idea for a moment. If Nikoli were a changed man, there would be no repercussions if he took the bait. If it was the old Nikoli, this time he had backup.

"Corporal Schmidt. Is what Nikoli says true? Have you been around enough to make that assertion? And correct me if I am wrong, have we not met him in the past?"

Schmidt approached the table. "I have known this man approximately three years. In that time, I have seen a dramatic change. He has been humbled and has learned to listen the hard way. If I would not have stepped in, Konstantin would have killed him with the help of Kirilli, Roman, and Sasha. That answers your first two questions. In regards to your third, the answer is…"

"You were at the train station were you not when we first came in contact with the Germans?"

"Correct."

Yakov let out a loud laugh. "This man is nothing more than a surrogate for Nikoli. I have heard enough of this foolishness. Nikoli is only trying to lull us back into his fold so he can reclaim what he lost. I have heard enough!"

Schmidt jumped across the table, pushing himself and Yakov to the floor. His left hand was tight around his throat. When Natashia recovered from the quickness of the attack and tried to intervene, a hard right sent her into the wall, plaster showering down upon her. Taras sat and watched.

"You will not question my motives, loyalty or honor, you filthy scum. I hold your life in my hands, and a slight twitch will separate your head from your body. Any other questions?"

Nikoli walked over and helped the stunned Natashia to her feet. "Corporal Schmidt. That will not be necessary. Please, release your grip and let him up. This is no way to build a trusting collaboration." He released Yakov and backed up.

"Yakov. You know me well enough to know that a few years ago I would have not given a second thought in letting him kill you. Agreed?"

He rubbed his sore, fragile neck. "Agreed," he choked out.

"Please, both of you retake your seats. There is much to discuss."

It took a few moments for the dust to clear and composures to be regained.

"As I was saying, I am a changed man. I have returned to enlist your help with a task I, nor this clan, can perform alone."

"And what would that be?" asked Yakov.

"If you remember, back in '40, Kirilli and I came across a camp the Germans were building by the old brewery."

"I remember. We made a strike on it."

"Correct. Since then, what we raided has quadrupled in size. It is not a prisoner of war camp or a training area for the German invaders. It is an extermination camp."

"What are they exterminating?" asked Natashia.

"Our food supply."

The answer took the three by surprise. "To what purpose are they doing this?" asked Yakov.

"They believe the Slavs, Jews, Gypsies, and other races that are not of Nordic, German ancestry are inferior and not worthy of walking the planet. Thus, they are rounding them up and killing them indiscriminately."

They absorbed the new information.

"I came back in hopes of recruiting as many as I can so we can attack the camp and release the captives."

Taras joined the discussion. "Who else do you have in mind?"

Nikoli sat back down. "There is only one place to go. Krakow."

"Who do we know there that would help? Jacub?"

"No."

"Then who?"

"Dmitri and Nicole."

\* \* \*

It was a taxing day. Dmitri spent the better half of it foraging the countryside for game to feed the twins, he and Nicole. It was becoming harder and harder each day. What the Germans had not confiscated or hunted the locals had. In time, he would either have to venture farther and farther out or move them to another location. Neither thought enticed him.

Nicole was exhausted when Dmitri returned. Between feeding and corralling the twins, she spent the rest of the day cleaning. She was lying in bed when she heard the back door shut hard.

"Dmitri. Is that you?" She heard something hit the clean floor. "Dmitri? I hope to hell you did not just drop a bloody carcass on my clean floor!" The only sound was that of boots coming towards the bedchamber. The door opened and Dmitri stood there, his clothes covered in blood and mud. She could see a clear path of muddy boot prints behind him.

"You ungrateful idiot!" she screamed. "I did not spend my day cleaning this pigpen so you could come trouncing in and destroy my work!" She rose from the bed, glaring at him.

"Here is what you are going to do. You are going to go outside, take off that filth you are wearing, and then you are going to clean up your mess. I cannot believe I agreed to mate with you. If my father would have given me a choice, I would have…"

"Done nothing, you spoiled brat! You will do as you are told and like it. That is what you will do. And remember this, you pampered princess. I am sick and tired of your incessant bickering and nagging. Ever since the boys were born you have been nothing but a major pain in my ass! I have done everything to make you comfortable, tend to your every need, help with the boys, and try to understand why you are such a bitch to me. I have had enough." He stomped his boots shaking globs of mud on the floor. "Furthermore, from this day forward, you will do as I say, when I say, and how I say I want it done. And right now, I want you to shut the hell up while I change. And tell the boys their dinner is in the back." He stomped off to his changing room, leaving a noticeable trail.

Fire flashed from her eyes. Her initial reaction was to tear him limb from limb. Then she thought about his words and the truth behind them. She agreed with everything he said except about being a bitch. She would get him to apologize for that or else.

"Boys. Come and get your dinner!"

\* \* \*

Two hours later, with the boys fed and sleeping, and the house back in order, they lay in bed. She had never seen him so distant. Not a word was spoken since he went to change. He stared at the ceiling, not acknowledging her. She rolled onto her left side, looking at him.

"Dmitri, my love. I want to apologize for my words and actions over the past months. I have come to realize how poorly I have treated you. I know you have done your best to provide for us and it has not been easy. I never once thought about the strain it has put on you. I want to thank you for taking care of us." Not a muscle on his face twitched. His eyes did not blink. They only stared at the ceiling.

"Dmitri! I am talking to you. Are you listening?" Nothing.

"Dmitri Boirarsky! I am trying to apologize to you! Do not ignore me."

He blinked then tilted his head to the right. "It is about damn time. I thought your mother was bad; I was wrong. You are just like her: impatient, arrogant, and whiny. It does not matter what I do or how much I do. It is never good enough, and I am sick of being treated as if I were nothing more than a doormat. Was it not enough I backed you when we told your mother to leave after the birth? Was it not enough to spend every waking moment hunting for you and the boys and nursing you back to health? Was it not enough I carried you and the boys when you wanted to give up on the way here? All I am received with, for my efforts, is a tirade about spilling mud and blood on the floor. Nicole, I am sick of it. And to be honest, there are many times I wish you would have died during the birthing so I could have a moment's rest." He turned his head and began staring at the ceiling again.

Anger welled up in her. She could feel the change beginning.

Dmitri heard the sounds and felt the bed moving. "The last time we changed in this room was to unite the clans. If you attempt it tonight, it will be the last change you ever make."

Her anger increased. Blood began leaking from the nail beds. Her mouth began contorting and shifting.

"I am warning you, Nicole."

A loud knock came from the front door. It was ignored as both were starting to change.

The banging became louder with a voice to accompany it. "Dmitri. Nicole. It is Nikoli. Come to the door now!"

They stared at each other, letting the anger subside. *Nikoli. What could he want?*

"Come to the door. We need to talk immediately!"

The changing stopped and normal features returned. They approached the door then opened it.

"Nikoli. What do you want?" asked Roman.

Nikoli could tell he came at the right time. The smell of changing hung heavy in the air and it was not that of melding.

"We have business to discuss and it cannot wait. May we come in?"

\* \* \*

For once, Dmitri was pleased to see Nikoli. What he interrupted could have been the demise of at least one of them or both.

They entered into the familiar drawing room, taking their respective seats.

"Nikoli. To what pleasure do we have with your untimely visit?" asked Dmitri.

"A matter that concerns us all. While you and Nicole have been away, much has changed. You already know about Svetlana and my situation. My brother has banished me from his clan, and the Germans are on the threshold of storming the ramparts of Stalingrad."

"How does this concern us?"

"If you remember, a year ago we raided the old brewery north of Krakow."

"Vaguely."

"The Germans have turned it into a camp with only one purpose, exterminating those they deem unworthy and a drag on their economy."

Dmitri was becoming bored. "Again, I do not see how this affects us."

In the past, Nikoli would have flown into a rage with Dmitri. Those days were gone.

"It affects all of us. One, it is our tried and true food supply they are disposing of for no reason other than hate. Once they have cleansed the ethnic races, it is difficult to know who will be next on the list, but I trust you, what the populace attempted in Kiev so many years ago, will become a reality. We will be next."

Dmitri was still not convinced.

"And what are you proposing to stop them?"

"We will attack the camp. Kill the guards and release all of the inmates."

Dmitri and Nicole began laughing, a reaction Nikoli was prepared for.

"And just how are you proposing to carry out this outlandish scheme? Before you answer, let me guess. What are there, seven of us? If I add in our sons, that makes a total of nine? Truly a force to be reckoned with."

"I realize your skepticism. Trust me, in time we will have enough to accomplish the goal."

"Trust you?" quipped Nicole, then stood up. "You are the last person any of us would trust, especially me. Do not think I have forgotten what it was like to live with you and watch you abuse and torment those surrounding you. You are the vilest creature I know, and I will have nothing to do with you!"

"I would expect nothing else. Give me time and you will see those days are gone."

"The only way you will be able to prove that to me is by killing yourself, and even that might not be enough." She sat back down, folding her arms.

Nikoli decided it was time for a change in tactics. He slammed his fist onto the desk, sending splinters flying.

"I have tried to reason with you two. I should have known better." His voice became louder. "Despite the past, I am still your father, and you will listen and obey me or suffer my wrath which you are familiar with!" He motioned for Yakov, Taras, Natashia, and Schmidt to move behind Dmitri and Nicole. They rose from their chairs.

"I have already admitted to my errors in the past presuming you would believe the change and accept my offer to join up." Fire began flashing in his eyes. "It appears that is not the case. Therefore, I have no choice but to resort to the old tactics you are so familiar with and force my will upon you." They both tried to stand up but were thrust back into their chairs. Nikoli jumped on the table. The sound of timbers and braces groaned under his weight. He stood half a meter from the two, glaring down. Blood and sweat began dripping on them. "I will ask one more time. Will you join me, or do you choose the alternative?"

Dmitri and Nicole looked at each other knowing what the alternative was.

They replied in unison, "Join."

## Chapter 26

## Final Act

**Univermag**
**January 1943**

The end was inevitable. The last emergency airfield was captured by the Russians. There was nothing left to fight for. His once-proud army was starved and out of hope. The only way out was to surrender with what dignity could be dredged up. He feared for his men falling into captivity knowing the Russian promises of medical care, good rations, and fair treatment were a fairy tale. He and his fellow soldiers brought an unwarranted amount of suffering and death to Russia, and a price would have to be paid. But it was a chance worth taking. If he refused, the only guarantee his men would receive was a bullet to the head or belly, or to become grease on a T-34s treads.

Each time he conferred with OKH requesting permission to cease hostilities, the answer was the same from Hitler. "NO! Under no circumstance will you lay down arms. You are ordered to fight to the last man and the last bullet. You are performing a vital act in tying up large formations the Russians could deploy to other fronts. Your efforts and sacrifice will guarantee our victory in the future."

What victory? Hitler said the war would be won in '42 and he and his men would return home heroes of the Reich. They would be allowed to rest and recuperate for the next campaign. Von Paulus, like many of his comrades, now knew that invading Russia was a colossal blunder, and no amount of propaganda could stop it. Even though his men were better trained, fed, and at one time supplied, there was one advantage they did not possess—an endless supply of manpower.

Von Paulus made one more plea to Hitler to surrender. The same reply was received, "NO!" Along with the response came a message informing him he was promoted to Field Marshall. It mattered not.

On January 31$^{st}$, von Paulus accepted the surrender terms. It was over. As he and Wilhelm walked to his car and captivity, an unearthly howl screamed in the distance.

* * *

Rudolph Gough dropped to his knees crying out.

## Chapter 27

## Westward

Zhukov, Khrushchev, and Chuikov stared at the ruins of the once-mighty city. They saluted the Hammer and Sickle flying over the square. None of them could fully embrace the devastation surrounding them. Burned-out tank hulks, fragments of men scattered about, damaged buildings as far they could see. There was not a pane of glass in any window. The buildings resembled extinct dinosaurs—empty and lifeless; nothing stirred in them. The only sound was that of rats scurrying through the ruins, fattening themselves on the carcasses of the dead and dying.

The initial losses were staggering. Over a million men and residents died in this cauldron of hell. That mattered none. What mattered was the complete and total defeat of the proud and mighty 6th Army. The defeat sent a message to the world that the Nazi war machine could, and would, be defeated. It would not be easy, but it was no longer an impossibility. Grit, determination, ruthlessness, and summary executions kept the men fighting. They were not as well trained as their opponent, but they had a resource the Germans never took into consideration, a seemingly unending resource of men.

"Comrade Zhukov. What are your thoughts on our great victory?"

"Comrade Stalin. It is a start. We have many battles ahead of us, but it is a start."

"Come now, Georgy. It is a great victory for our people. We destroyed one of the greatest armies on the face of the earth, and are at this time sending ninety thousand of them to our camps in Siberia. Our great win has opened up the entire Ukraine. There is nothing to stop us from kicking the invaders out by the end of the year."

"Comrade Stalin. I find it prudent to remind you Leningrad is still under siege, and the enemy is only one hundred and twenty kilometers from Moscow. If we would have moved faster and trapped Army Group A in the Caucasus Mountains, I would tend to agree with your assessment. As it is, we have much more work to do until all of our lands are free."

Stalin frowned with the history lecture.

"Comrade Chuikov. What are your thoughts on the matter?"

"Comrade Stalin. It has been a long four months. The issues you speak of are beyond my knowledge. I will agree with you both; we have and will defeat the Germans in time. Until then, I request to be excused so I may celebrate with my comrades and then rest."

He saluted then walked off to his headquarters, still in the hill of the bank of the Volga.

"Comrade Zhukov. I will expect the fall of Kharkov in the coming months. See to it."

He too left.

Zhukov had already issued the order to drive on Kharkov in hopes von Manstein would not be able to maintain an orderly retreat and regroup. Rokossovsky's army had enough fuel and ammunition to reach the city, but it would be risky. It would require luck, audacity, and a solid supply line. The first two were not a problem. If an early thaw arrived, even with the wide tracks on the T-34s, they would consume more fuel and the trucks carrying the fuel would also bog down in the mire. He could use the railways, but the Germans would destroy every kilometer they could as they retreated. All the storehouses and stations would be burned to the ground and reduced to rubble. The engineer battalions were ordered at times to outpace the forward elements and begin all necessary repairs immediately.

A sharp north wind rifled through his bones and filled his nose with the rancid smell of burnt flesh.

*I have one more debt to pay.* He went to his car.

"Driver, take me to Gumrak."

\* \* \*

Konstantin, Kirilli, and Roman could not believe what they witnessed over the last month. It was their detachment that captured the airfields at Pitomnik and Gumrak, sealing the fate of those trapped in the hollowed-out city. No more supplies would come in, and no more wounded would be transported out. What stunned them and their clans was the carnage they came across. Never in their centuries of warfare had they witnessed such a decimation of men. Thousands littered the tarmac and surrounding areas. Many were frozen to death. Others moaned and screamed as limbs were severed and tossed aside to be burned for warmth. The air was putrid with the stench of burning, rotting, dying flesh. Those who were still alive but incapable of moving, were succumbing to the infestation of lice feeding on them. Some cases were so bad, they could see the uniforms moving from the unseen army.

They were not strangers to war by any means, but this new mechanized warfare was a thrill incomparable to anything they could imagine. Guttenberg had trained them well, and when the order to attack was issued, it was fast, frightening, and perfect. Each command the general issued was followed to the T and the results were devastatingly exciting. They mourned the loss of the blood spilling on their soil, but they relished in the tactic of crushing the enemy with no remorse and wanting more. They were beginning to grasp twentieth-century technology and its advantages.

They now stood shoulder-to-shoulder at the airfield with their tanks in parade formation preparing to be awarded the Order of Lenin by Marshall Georgy Zhukov!

\* \* \*

After the ceremony, Georgy invited the three to join him for a toast. Each man was given a tumbler full of vodka. He was not sure they would accept since he knew of their lineage.

"To our *motherland*, gentlemen." He downed his shot and the others followed.

He poured another.

"To the day when all the fascists are expelled from our country!"

He poured another.

"And for those who are not expelled, may their corpses fertilize our fields for a bountiful harvest!"

Again, all three followed his lead, but not as enthusiastically.

As he began to pour another round, Konstantin stopped him.

"Georgy. We have been friends far too long for the charade to continue. We could drain the entire bottle and it will not affect us. This, you know, so why the act?"

He downed another shot then sat down.

"I was not disregarding our arrangement, only trying to soften it."

"Why? Are we not men who speak their minds?"

"We are."

"Then speak."

He waited a few seconds before continuing. "During our victorious battle, General Chuikov informed me of unnatural events in the city. At first, I dismissed the reports as unreliable until the frequency increased with each week. The bodies of Russian and German soldiers were found completely dismembered with all of their blood drained. I instructed Chuikov to keep a separate file for only our eyes, and to instruct his men not to ask questions but stay focused on the task at hand. My first instinct was that you and your kind were raiding the city. I cast that idea aside when I realized even you are not capable of such barbarity."

"Trust me, none of my clan has stepped foot in the city." He looked at Kirilli and Roman.

"What do you know of these events our friend speaks of?'

"We know nothing," replied Roman.

"Are you sure the reports you received are accurate?" asked Konstantin.

"The most current and accurate ones came from Vasily Zaytsev."

"I have heard of him." Replied Konstantin.

"Yes, I have heard of him. Top sniper in Stalingrad." Interjected Roman.

"Correct. His observations and notes kept us well apprised of the German positions and defenses. He is an honest man, but when he dictated his reports, the look in his eyes was that of confusion as if he were looking past the present and seeing something he could not believe or accept. Based on that, is it possible there is a splinter group you are not aware of?"

He pondered the thought for a moment. "None I can think of. Kirilli, Roman, what do you think?'

"All I know is, it was not one of us," sounded off Roman.

Kirilli paced the room, muttering.

"Something to add, Kirilli?"

"Initially, I would blame Nikoli for such a heinous act, but to what end. Then there are Dmitri and Nicole. Yet, after careful consideration, that is not possible with her having young ones. She and he would be more involved with caring for the newborns. That leaves only one candidate—Svetlana."

"Why would she be here?"

"That I cannot answer. Nikoli did banish her, and she was last seen walking to the east with Dina."

"Where would they go?"

"Since she was pregnant, she would need help with the delivery or she and the child would surely die, leaving Dina on her own. Of which, I doubt she would last long." He studied the question a bit longer. "There is only one place that might provide her shelter, but it is a long shot and over one thousand kilometers from here. I cannot believe they could have traveled this far in such a short time."

"Where, Kirilli?"

"A town on the east side of the Urals. One where no mortal venture, and if they do, never leave." He paused for a moment then shook his head. "The thought is absurd and most unlikely."

"Well, there is something out there, and I fear we have not seen or heard the last of it," replied Georgy. "I must return to my headquarters and continue planning. If any of you find out anything, you know how to reach me." He left the room.

Five minutes later while the three discussed the issue, a low piercing howl was heard from the northeast.

* * *

Otto found a fresh uniform and changed into it. The old one was covered with blood, brains, and other human fragments. When the Russians made their final push to take back the city, he went into a feeding frenzy. Elizabeth joined him, caught up in the excitement. Dina, Svetlana, and Gough kept their distance picking up what was left over. The savagery of the two appalled the other three.

Svetlana could not believe she had birthed a monster such as Elizabeth. Since she and Otto had merged, there was no controlling her. She realized Elizabeth's earlier threats were not idle and if she and her splinter group wished to remain with the living, they needed to slip away.

"Dina, it is time to leave."

"To where?"

"Anywhere but here. If we do not leave now, we may not see tomorrow."

"What about him?"

"We will take him along for the moment. He may be of use."

\* \* \*

It was a feeding frenzy never seen before. Otto and Elizabeth slashed, dismembered, and feasted on the fleeing, defeated, demoralized Germans. Many were past the point of caring. Four months of freezing temperatures, empty bellies, and no hope took a heavy toll. They blankly stared as their bodies were ripped apart. Some made an attempt to flee, but to where? Others with still some fight in them tried to ward off the attackers with a final hurrah for the Führer, but to no avail. Their bones and fragments were tossed aside as the two continued their rampage.

They did not only target Germans. As the advance guards of the Russians approached, they too were not immune to the carnage.

After two hours of feeding, the pair trekked off to the northwest, proud of their accomplishment.

Elizabeth wiped the blood from her face, spitting out flesh from her teeth. "Otto. Together we can rule the world. No one can stand in our path. We are invincible!"

He finished draining the last body then discarded it. "You are correct as long as you remember your place."

"My place?"

He slapped her, sending her sprawling five meters."

"Your place! It is by my side and under my shadow. I am the ultimate, super soldier! I was designed for a purpose, but now that has changed. My masters thought they could control me. They thought wrong. I will answer to no man or creature on this earth. I am Otto the Invincible!"

She stood up, gaining her senses. "I too am an abomination. Together, there is nothing we cannot achieve!"

"On that point you are correct." He looked to the west. "Before we rule and take our rightful place as masters over these pathetic humans, I need to visit those who built me. I want to thank them in person before I take my rightful place as their true master."

His body began changing again as he worked himself into a fury.

"I will thank the Reichsführer personally and his stooge Adolf for ripping me from my family along with all the others." Fangs began protruding. Blood seeped out of nail beds.

"They wanted a super soldier who would be obedient and bow to their wishes. NEVER!"

Coarse hair began covering his body. The new tunic began ripping apart as his muscles and sinew grew and contorted.

His eyes flashed red, green, and blue fire. His voice was raspy and hard. "They are FOOLS! And I shall show them what a superior being is capable of performing! It is not to obey a useless ideology or flag or mystical beliefs. It is to rule with brutal force and will!"

Elizabeth could feel her own transformation coming on with his excitement.

"But first, I have another need to tend to." He turned to Elizabeth. "You!"

He let out a horrific howl as he took her partially transformed body.

# Chapter 28

# Kharkov

The next six weeks saw no rest for the weary. Per Comrade, Stalin, Zhukov pushed his army to the breaking point in hopes of being able to crush what resistance the Germans could muster. He would drive on Belgorod, Kursk, and Kharkov, then drive his southern arm to the axis of Dnepropetrovsk-Melitopol, cutting off the retreating Army Group A and ending the conflict in the south. It was a bold strategy, but well worth the gamble.

Initially, the plan started off with excellent results. Golikov, Vatutin, and Reiter ripped through the thin German lines gaining kilometer after kilometer. Despite the heady advance, what Zhukov feared was coming to bear. His troops were understrength, supply could not keep up, and fresh replacements divisions were taking too long to form. The only plus, the weather was cooperating. The ground remained frozen allowing his forces to keep up the pace.

In late February, the front line reports were dimming his optimism; the Germans were reforming and putting up stiff resistance. On March 5th, his temperament changed. The 3rd Tank Army had been mauled south of Kharkov and was in full flight. The situation began to deteriorate. On March 6th, von Manstein's forces crossed the Mosh River and were poised to thrust north and retake Kharkov. When word reached him the 69th and 40th Armies were split in two, he realized there would be no more offensive actions in the south, and he would have to take the defensive for the moment. His attempts to rally the troops and set up solid defensive positions in and around Kharkov failed. There were not enough troops or fuel to stop the onslaught of the

4th Panzer Army. Von Manstein surprised him with not only a valiant defensive plan, but his ability to muster the forces to strike hard and send his troops reeling was impressive.

Stalin berated him when he heard that Kharkov had fallen again along with Belgorod. Zhukov took the criticism in stride. Yes, the Germans had managed a victory of sorts. In the broader scheme, they had lost over one hundred and fifty thousand men and an untold amount of irreplaceable equipment and material. And their advance created a huge bulge in the Russian lines, which would be an ideal location to launch his summer offensive, or wait for the Germans to attack the ripe, tempting apple in his lines.

For the first time since June of '42, the sounds of battle were absent. The cries of the wounded and dying no longer filled the night air, whether natural or not. The eerie calm that replaced the familiar sounds filled many with an uneasy calm. Both sides needed the break to reflect on the carnage of the last nine months. Many spent their time remembering lost comrades while being thankful they were still alive. Some took the time to write letters home and think of better times, while others stared blankly into the vast expanse of nothingness wondering what awaited them.

# Chapter 29

# Accountability

**Berlin**
**March 15th**

Goebbels, Goering, Keitel, Bormann, and Himmler were summoned to a meeting. No one knew why they were called, but they could guess. The defeat at Stalingrad was not news for the masses. It was an internal matter that would be addressed when the Führer decided the time was right.

Each one was required to show identification at the gates. If one complained or asked the guard if they knew who they were, the response was the same, "By order of the Führer." They begrudgingly pulled out their IDs and presented them.

Keitel was the first to enter. When he tried to sit at the head of the table, the guard waved him off, putting him at the end.

Next came Goering, Himmler, and Goebbels. The men sat in silence, lost in their own thoughts. Five minutes passed before the silence was broken.

"Does anyone know why we are here?" asked Goering.

"Because of your failure," replied Keitel.

Goering's face turned beet red. "My failure! My failure? Do you know how many of your soldiers my Luftwaffe evacuated from your failed offensive?"

"Failed offensive? If your Luftwaffe would have delivered the promised seven hundred tonnes a day, and not the paltry one fifty to two hundred, we would have won. But like Dunkirk, you overreached and failed."

"I did not fail! Once again, your armies were poorly led and trained. It was the Wehrmacht's incompetence that cost us victory. My pilots knocked out communication hubs, disrupted logistical lines, and kept the enemy's heads low. All your troops had to do was follow our lead and defeat the demoralized units. Instead, your men sat back, smoking and drinking, allowing the enemy to regroup."

Keitel shot up from his chair. "Listen to me, you obese, pompous, drug addict! My armies have moved faster and conquered more territory in three short years than any other army in the annals of history! And remember this, you lard of blubber, my army followed the orders issued by the Führer. To ridicule and blame my armies for your incompetence is blaming Hitler's direct orders!" He sat back down. Goering uncomfortably shifted in his chair.

"Gentlemen. As the Minister of Propaganda, it is not wise for us to quibble over past events. While both of you are correct to a degree, I assure you, it would be wise to accept your failures rather than look for blame. Since I am the voice of Germany, the people will believe any and everything I say. To ensure your place in the hierarchy, I suggest when the Führer enters, you apologize to him and have a plan for redeeming your graces. I see no other way."

They both stared at him. "I will not have a cripple dictate policy to the Chief Officer of the Army. I suggest you stay in your safe room and continue to spout off your ridiculous rhetoric no one with a brain listens to. When I think of your Christmas broadcast concerning the troops trapped in Stalingrad, I still laugh. Telling the people our troops are sitting around Christmas trees laughing, singing, and handing out presents over steins of beer with full bellies, when in reality they were freezing to death living on horse and rat meat. The only drinking they did was from the snow they melted. A fine Christmas indeed!"

"It is my job to instill the people with confidence and keep morale up. Look how many blankets, pajamas, heavy overcoats, and fur-lined boots were donated to the cause."

"And how many of those precious items reached my troops? None, because Herr Meyer's air force and Himmler's SS did not properly protect our supply lines. Instead, they were destroyed by partisans. The bulk of what you collected is still warehoused in depots behind the lines or were burned in the boxcars by partisans. What they did not burn, they took for themselves. Job well done, Joseph."

"It is my job to gather the items you need. Not the transportation or protection of them. In that, the failure falls on all of you."

"Typical political response, empty and useless," scoffed Keitel.

"General, let me remind you; my speeches are authorized by the Führer. If you have a problem with what I say, perhaps you should voice your concerns to him." Keitel settled down.

They stewed in their thoughts waiting for their Führer.

Another five minutes passed.

\* \* \*

The door opened and Hitler, flanked by Bormann, entered. All four men stood up and saluted, "Heil, Hitler." He did not acknowledge their presence and proceeded to the front of the table.

As the four began sitting down, he spoke. "Remain standing!" He kept his back to them for at least two minutes. His was slightly slumped over, with a noticeable shake. He began turning around. His eyes bored into each man at the same time.

"You lied to me. Each and every one of you lied to me." The tone was flat, controlled, yet filled with anger. "All of you. The leaders of your respective departments, lied to me." The tone became louder and more unrestrained. "Me! Your Führer! The hope of Germany. You…" he began pointing at them, "lied to me. Adolf Hitler. The great leader of Germany. You not only lied but have betrayed me with your treacherous plots." Sweat began building on his brow. Spittle frothed from his mouth. "For the last ten minutes, I have heard every word you spoke! How dare you! How dare any of you question my orders and motives. How dare you! What gives you the right to question anything I say or do? Was it not I who put you in power? Was it not I who dismantled the Versailles Treaty? Was it not I who took back the Ruhr Valley, annexed Austria, reclaimed the Sudetenland, eliminated Poland, crushed France, isolated England, sealed off the Scandinavian countries, and have our forces standing on the banks of the Volga?" He pounded on the table; sweat began saturating his shirt and tunic. His black hair covered his right eye. "I am the one who rebuilt Germany. No one else was capable of such a monumental task. When the war is won, history will remember me, and only me. You will all be forgotten unless I find it in my graces to mention your feeble contributions to my Third Reich. MY THIRD REICH!" Over the years, they were accustomed to his outbreaks and hysterical behavior, but never was it directed at them. They quaked in their boots at rigid attention knowing he could have them shot on sight or worse.

"None of you are immune. All of you are guilty of treachery, and in the end, you will pay for your crimes against me and the German people. The only chance you have of staying in power is by impressing me and proving you are worthy to serve. Goering, Keitel is correct in his assessment of the Luftwaffe's performance over the past few years. You failed at Dunkirk, Stalingrad, and over Germany. Each night the RAF bombs our cities at will, and soon the Americans will be bombing in numbers during the day. You are no longer allowed to speak in public congratulating yourself or the Luftwaffe. If not for your incompetence, the British would have been forced to surrender and the swastika would be flying over Stalingrad. The only pluses for you are the performances in Poland, France, and the Demyansk pocket. General Keitel, the only reason you are still alive is that von Manstein was able to repulse the Russians from Kharkov and Belgorod allowing us an excellent jump off position for the summer offensives. You failed to knock Leningrad out in '41 and '42. I should court-martial you for losing my 6$^{th}$ Army! How dare you use inferior Rumanian and Italian forces to protect our flanks. What were you thinking? I will answer that!" He pointed a finger at him. "Because you are incompetent as are the generals under your command. From this day forward, all military decisions will be made by me! I am the Führer and I, unlike you, will lead our armies to victory!" He sat down catching his breath, brushing the hair from his eyes.

"Sit down," he quietly said.

He looked up, fire and hate still filling his eyes.

"Gentlemen, fail me again and pay the price. We are Germany, and the word failure is not in our vocabulary. My destiny is to save the world from the Jews and any other mediocre race. I will not be denied my divine destiny. Understood?"

"Jawohl, Mein Führer," came the answer in unison.

"Good. Keitel, you, Bormann, and Goering may leave. Remember what I said."

The three saluted and exited.

"Heinrich, I did not want the others to hear what I have to say. Joseph, nothing what we talk about leaves this room. I am disappointed with your security efforts with regard to our supply lines. I cannot tie up the Wehrmacht or the fighting SS divisions performing these tasks. You must tighten up your security units and put an end to this. In '41 we lost a convoy. In '42 a minor railroad station was destroyed. Along with that, the raid on the rail depot in Kharkov was disastrous to say the least. And, need I remind you of the catastrophe at Bataysk?"

"Nein, Mein Führer."

"Good. Good, my faithful Heinrich."

"Joseph. Has there been any mention of these acts to the public?"

"Nein, Mein Führer."

"Excellent. Very good. Now, Heinrich. What do we know of Otto?"

"The last report from von Paulus gave me the belief that he was operating on his own."

"I see."

"Joseph. If he were captured, do you believe the Russians would have broadcast his capture?"

"Only if he revealed himself, Mein Führer."

"Excellent. Those are my thoughts also. That would lead us to believe he is still alive. Heinrich, find him."

"Jawohl, Mein Führer."

The hour grows late. Therefore, I suggest you dine with me this evening."

"It would be my pleasure, Mein Führer."

"And Heinrich."

"Yes, Mein Führer."

"Do find the lad."

# Glossary

## Definitions

1. Raush — move, hurry up
2. Danke — thank you
3. Fraulein — Miss
4. Jawohl — yes
5. Frau — Mrs.
6. Hofbrau — a bar
7. Heil — hail to
8. Guten abend — good evening
9. Wehrmacht — German regular army
10. Mein Gott — My God
11. Wie gehts — how are you
12. Wo ist — Where is
13. Was ist los — What is going on.
14. Verstehen — Understood
15. Gott mit us — God go with us
16. Mein Kampf — My Struggle
17. Verstehen — Understood
18. OKH — High Command of the German Army

19. Weimar Republic   The                 ruling government until Hitler took power in 1933

20. Luftwaffe          air force

21. Kriegsmarine       navy

22. Sterbenhilfe       mercy killing

23. Untermenschen      sub-human

## Metric Conversions

1. Kilogram         2.2 pounds

2. Kilometer        0.62 miles

3. Meter            3.28 feet

4. Liter            0.26 gallons

5. Centimeter       2.54 inches

6. Millimeter       0.10 centimeters

## **Pronunciations:**

1. Boirarsky — Bor-ar-sky
2. Bezpieczenstwo — Bech-piench-ens-tvo
3. M-Spartanin — She-ar-tani
4. Walensa — Valensa
5. Tatra — same
6. Beskid Slaski — Besh-kid Slahs-ki
7. Bieszczedy — Bien-sh-chendy
8. Belovezh — Ben-loen-zh
9. Miechow — Mien-hohv
10. Nowy-Sacz — Nohv-eh Sach
11. Wolbrum — Vol-broom
12. Trzyciaz — Tr-sey-chiah-zh
13. Myslowice — Meh-slov-ichen
14. Tychy — Yeh-heh
15. Chrzano — Hr-zh-ahn-oh
16. Wadowice — Vahd-o-vichen
17. Wewelsburg — Vev-els-burg
18. Schmeisser — same
19. Reichsführer — Rikes-fure-er

If you enjoyed the story, please do not hesitate to post a review on Amazon, Goodreads or any other site of preference.

Other works include:
Gateway: Pioche, Science fiction
Destination D.C. Book two of the Gateway series
Target Berlin Book three of the Gateway series
Occupation, WWII Alternative history
Sabotage Book two
Terror at the Sterling, horror
Love's True Second Chance, Memoir
Why Did Everything Happen?, Memoir
The Baseball Coaching Manual: Little League to High School. Volumes I & II, Instructional
Goober and Bill, Humor
Final Delivery, Suspense short
Women of War-poetry
Irving Titans-NFL satire

Other works available through LDDJ Enterprises Publishing
Angelic Answers: Love Letter for Daily Life, Kathryn Magee, Spiritual

You can follow me at:
Twitter: @Jeff Dawson59
Facebook: https://www.facebook.com/jeff.dawson.184 or https://www.facebook.com/pages/Loves-True-Second-Chance/201274679901838
Facebook: https://www.facebook.com/pages/Why-did-everything-happen/146270185426560?ref=hl
Website: http://jeff-dawson.blogspot.com/
Email: LDDJEnterprises@gmail.com

Amazon link: http://www.amazon.com/Jeff-Dawson/e/B0054DRYIO/ref=sr_tc_2_0?qid=1394463163&sr=1-2-ent

www.ingramcontent.com/pod-product-compliance
Lightning Source LLC
LaVergne TN
LVHW051115080426
835510LV00018B/2055